Weaving Well-Being

3rd Class
Positive Emotions
Teacher Resource Book

by Fiona Forman & Mick Rock

Weaving Well-Being

THE MORE YOU WEAVE...
THE BETTER YOU FEEL!

Acknowledgements and thanks

The authors would like to thank the principals, teachers and pupils of the following schools for their support, co-operation and encouragement in piloting these materials:

Pope John Paul II NS, Malahide, Co. Dublin

Donabate - Portrane Educate Together NS, Donabate, Co. Dublin

Balbriggan Educate Together NS, Balbriggan, Co. Dublin

Balrothery NS, Balbriggan, Co. Dublin

St. Martin de Porres NS, Tallaght, Dublin 24

Sincere thanks also to:

Ciara Garland

Mary Carroll

Siobhan O'Brien

Stephanie Cronin

Mike Egan

Linda Rock

Emmet Murphy

Matthew Boyd

Andrea Heron

Rebecca Lemaire

Tomasz Piwowarczyk

Outside the Box Learning Resources Ltd.

Weaving Well-Being – Positive Emotions – Teacher Resource Book

Written by: Fiona Forman & Mick Rock
Edited by: Outside The Box Learning Resources Ltd.
Design and Layout by: Andrea Heron
Illustrations by: Andrea Heron, Rébecca Lemaire, Emmet Murphy, et al.
Photography by: Tomasz Piwowarczyk

Published in Ireland by: Outside The Box Learning Resources Ltd.
W6W Tougher's Business Park, Newhall, Naas, Co. Kildare W91 YR82, Ireland.
Tel: 045 409322 (+353 45 409322). Fax: 045 409959 (+353 45 409959).

Email: info@otb.ie www.otb.ie

ISBN: 978-1-906926-46-5

Weaving Well-Being

THE MORE YOU WEAVE... THE BETTER YOU FEEL!

Contents

Part 1:
Introduction to
Weaving Well-Being

About the Authors

•

Background to Programme

•

Aims of the Programme

•

Teacher Well-Being

•

What SPHE strands and strand units are covered?

•

Structure and Methodologies

About the Authors

Fiona Forman

Fiona is a Primary School Teacher from Dublin. She graduated from St. Patrick's College, Dublin in 1987 and since then has taught all class levels, including resource and learning support. She holds an honours B.Ed. Degree and a Diploma in Montessori Education. She has worked as a Teaching Practice supervisor of student teachers of St. Patrick's College, Dublin. Fiona is also a trained and experienced facilitator of the Rainbows programme which supports children who have experienced loss.

Fiona's keen interest in children's well-being and mental health led her to undertake a M.Sc. in Applied Positive Psychology (MAPP) with the University of East London. As a result of her studies, she began to introduce practical and child-centred Positive Psychology concepts into her classroom, with highly positive feedback from children and parents alike. She then began her collaboration with co-author Mick Rock on the creation of the **Weaving Well-Being** programme.

Fiona has delivered talks on children's well-being to teachers and parents. She has spoken about her classroom experience and research at Féilte (A Celebration of Teaching and Learning). She is a regular media contributor on her experience of putting well-being and mental health at the heart of the classroom.

Fiona is also the mother of two teenage children. She feels passionate about equipping children with evidence-based life-skills to allow them to develop resilience and to thrive and flourish.

Mick Rock

Mick is a qualified Executive and Life Coach and a Motivational Speaker who has helped hundreds of people to enhance their lives and achieve a wide variety of goals. As the parent of two sons, Mick is extremely passionate about working with and helping children to deal with the various challenges in their lives, to increase their happiness and well-being and to fulfil their true potential.

Mick has a wide range of qualifications in the area of Personal Development. He completed a three year M.Sc. in Applied Positive Psychology with the University of East London (with distinction). His final dissertation was a research project on the use of Positive Psychology Interventions in Primary Schools.

Together with his wife Linda, who is a Primary School Teacher, he set up New Horizons Montessori School in 2002 and this has become established as one of the leading Montessori Schools in North Dublin. He has worked with children's charities and served as the Chairperson of the Board of Management of a Primary School for four years.

Mick is also the owner of Act Now, a company that delivers motivational talks, training programmes and one to one coaching to adult participants. These sessions have a strong focus on Positive Psychology Interventions. Before setting up Act Now he held various management roles including five years as Training and Development Manager within the financial services sector.

Background to Programme

What is Well-Being?

'A state of Well-Being in which the individual realises his or her own abilities; can cope with the normal stresses of life; can work productively and fruitfully and is able to make a contribution to his or her own community'.

This is the definition of well-being outlined by the DES in their 2015 *Guidelines for Mental Health Promotion; Well-Being in Primary Schools.*

A more child centred definition of well-being is used throughout this programme as follows:

> "Well-being means feeling good and strong in our minds and bodies, having energy, getting along with and helping others, knowing our strengths and feeling proud because we are doing our best. It means we can cope with the little problems and disappointments of life. It means enjoying life, being grateful for what we have and accepting ourselves just as we are!"

A Self-Assessment Check-Up Table, using indicators based on this definition is provided at the back of the children's Activity Book. A copy is also included in this Teacher Resource Book (SW8 - page 69). This is an optional tool that can be used by each teacher at their discretion.

Weaving Well-Being is an SPHE programme designed to teach children skills and strategies which develop positive mental health, and so promote well-being, in accordance with this definition. The skills are based on current research from the field of Positive Psychology.

Child's art showing one of the elements of well-being.

Framework of the Weaving Well-Being Programme

The chart below shows the main topics included in the full programme from second to sixth class. Due to the overlap of strands and strand units in the SPHE curriculum, there is room for a certain amount of flexibility regarding the suitability of the lessons for different class levels. Teachers could also decide to use the lessons in different year levels based on the specific needs and abilities of their individual classes.

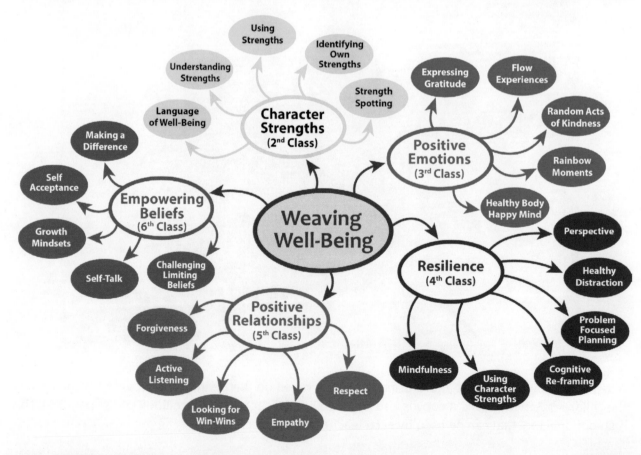

What is Positive Psychology?

Positive Psychology is a relatively new branch of psychology. It was founded by Professor Martin Seligman, a professor at the University of Pennsylvania, in 1998. Seligman observed that psychology up to that point was deficit based and overly focused on mental ill-health. He identified the need for more focus and research on the components of mental well-being. Therefore, Positive Psychology is the science of well-being, personal growth and resilience. It is founded on the concept of identifying and developing personal strengths, as opposed to correcting deficits. Positive Psychology uses evidence-based activities which help people not only to cope with everyday stresses but to flourish, grow and engage with life on an optimal level, whenever possible.

The lessons and activities in this programme are guided by Seligman's P.E.R.M.A. theory of well-being. The P.E.R.M.A. model identifies five particular components of well-being: *Positive Emotions, Engagement using Character Strengths, Relationships, Meaning and Achievement.*

Weaving Well-Being introduces children to many Positive Psychology strategies and activities which can empower them to become active participants in creating, maintaining and boosting positive mental health throughout their lives.

The third class programme consists of ten lessons which are designed to teach five specific evidence-based strategies to boost positive emotions on a daily basis. These are:

- practising gratitude
- understanding and developing flow experiences
- counteracting the negativity bias
- practising kindness
- keeping physically healthy

Page taken from the accompanying Positive Emotions Pupil Activity Book

The benefits of including specific well-being lessons in our classrooms

The **Weaving Well-Being** programme is designed to support and improve children's well-being across a number of areas - social, emotional, physical and psychological. Nurturing children's well-being in these areas can lead to increased academic performance, positive behaviour and better life outcomes[1].

Children today face a wide range of challenges which have a significant impact on their well-being and this is demonstrated by research completed in this area. One study showed that 2% of children aged 5 to 15 experienced a major depression[2] and another found that 14% of young people suffer from anxiety.[3] The increase in anxiety and depression in young children also leads to delays in treatments with a recent HSE report[4] showing that there was an 11% increase in the demand for mental health services and that 42% of children and adolescents have been waiting in excess of 6 months for access to these services.

At the same time there are wide ranges of positive psychology tools available which have a significant and increasing amount of empirical evidence that supports their effectiveness in enhancing well-being and reducing anxiety and depression.[5] Often children have to wait until adulthood before being introduced to interventions that could potentially enhance their lives in a number of ways.

School is an appropriate setting for children to grow and become empowered instead of focusing on stresses and challenges. Teachers are ideally placed to teach these interventions to children and to enable them to reap the benefits at the earliest possible stage.

It must be added that enhancing children's well-being can also lead to a range of other benefits including increased academic performance. For example, cultivating positive emotions can improve performance by enhancing attention and creativity.[6] Other research has shown that happy people are more creative, can multi-task better, are more tolerant of boring tasks and are more helpful and sociable.[7]

Anxiety in Children

Anxiety is a common and growing issue for children. Positive emotions have been linked to the development of resilience.[17] By encouraging children to boost their positive emotions daily, the benefits of the Positivity Ratio in buffering against the effects of negative emotions such as anxiety can be enhanced.[33] By encouraging such a proactive approach to developing well-being, children's self-efficacy can be developed. Self-efficacy is the belief a person has in their own abilities to deal with problems or difficulties and it is strongly linked to well-being. Self-efficacy is further explored and developed in the **Weaving Well-Being Tools of Resilience** Programme which is aimed at fourth class.

The Importance of a Whole School Culture of Well-Being

Research shows that in addition to teaching children the specific skills of well-being, having a whole school culture of well-being optimises the benefits to the whole school community.[8] Such a culture includes the following characteristics:

- the presence of strong positive relationships[9]

- a sense of belonging and shared identity[10]

- appreciation and valuing of academic and non-academic achievements[11]

- a participative approach to the management of the school in which the student voice is heard[11]

- clear rules and high expectations conveyed to students[11]

- students' needs for autonomy, competence and relatedness being met[12]

This programme is specifically designed to support a whole school approach by providing a spiral curriculum of well-being which can be delivered within Primary Schools.

Part 1
Introduction to Weaving Well-Being

Aims of the Programme

The aim of ***Weaving Well-Being*** is to allow children to learn about and practise the specific behaviours and activities which have been linked to Well-Being, in a child-centred, interesting and age-appropriate way. The children are encouraged to practise the skills, strategies and activities, to see how they feel and how useful they find them. Children will have individual preferences for specific activities. It is helpful to expose them to a wide variety so that they can find a range of strategies which best suit their particular personality. Weaving Well-being provides a concrete and practical method to incorporate positive mental health strategies into the classroom.

In this way, children learn how to become creators of their own well-being - over the course of the programme they learn how to weave all of the elements of well-being into their everyday life. They continually reflect on how the interventions make them feel.

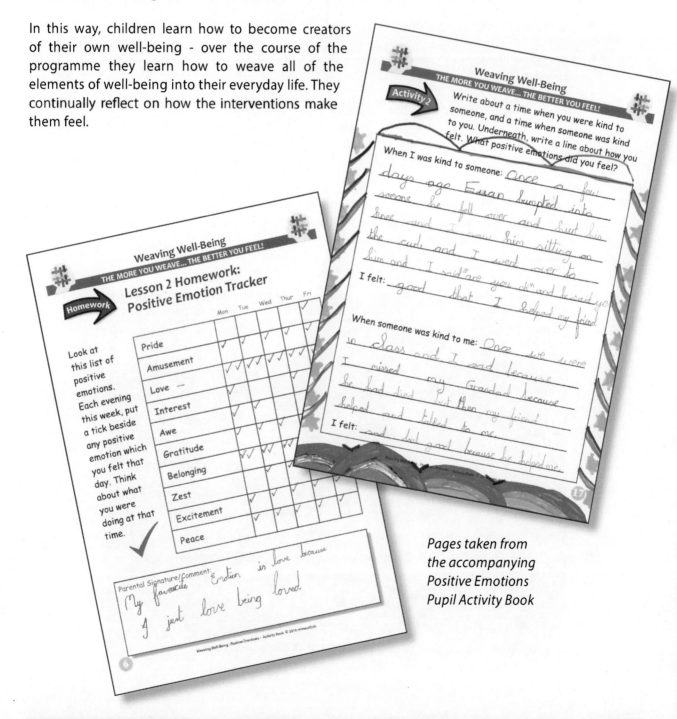

Pages taken from the accompanying Positive Emotions Pupil Activity Book

Teacher Well-Being

It is recognised that teachers face a wide range of challenges in their own lives and that teaching is in itself, a very demanding role. Any initiatives that can help teachers deal more effectively with these challenges will be extremely beneficial. Introducing well-being lessons into schools is an excellent opportunity to enhance teacher well-being at the same time.

Many of the activities included in each year of the *Weaving Well-Being* programme have been researched in the adult population as well and have been shown to provide a wide range of benefits. These can often be implemented in the same way as used by the children or may need slight adaptation to make them more relevant to teachers or other adults.

For example in Lesson 7, children are introduced to the concept of *Rainbow Moments*. These moments relate to the little parts of our day where things go well for us. Our brains naturally look for bad things in our day and spotting our "*Rainbow Moments*" can help re-train our brains to notice and pay attention to the small, simple, positive things that occur on a daily basis. We as adults can equally benefit from re-training our brains to pay attention to what is already good in our lives.

Therefore, it is strongly advised that, as teachers deliver this programme, they look for opportunities to complete and benefit from activities they feel are most relevant to them. During each lesson teachers should have two roles:

> **1.** As a teacher introducing children to each concept and encouraging them to complete the various activities and homework to help them obtain the maximum benefits from each lesson.

> **2.** As a learner, looking to see what they can learn from each lesson and how they can personally implement each tool.

Teacher well-being is also enhanced by the presence of a whole-school culture of well-being (see previous section on "Whole School Culture" - page 9).

What SPHE strands and strand units are covered?

The lessons are designed to be implemented within the framework of the SPHE curriculum. They tie-in with stated aims of the third and fourth class curriculum under the strands units of:

Strand: Myself

- Self-identity

- Taking care of my body

- Growing and changing

- Making decisions

Strand: Myself and others

- My friends and other people

- Relating to others

The specific strand and strand unit for each lesson is included at the start of each lesson plan.

Overview of SPHE Strands and Strand Units Covered:

Strand	Strand Unit	Lesson Plans
Myself	Self-identity - *Self-awareness* - *Developing self-confidence*	1, 2, 3, 6, 7 and 8 2 and 9
Myself	Taking care of my body - *Health and well-being*	1, 2, 3, 6, 7 and 8
Myself	Growing and changing - *As I grow I change* - *Feelings and emotions*	1, 3, 5, 6, 7 and 8 1, 2, 3, 5 and 6
Myself	Making decisions	1, 3, 9 and 10
Myself and others	My friends and other people	4, 5, 6 and 7
Myself and others	Relating to others	4, 6 and 7

Structure and Methodologies

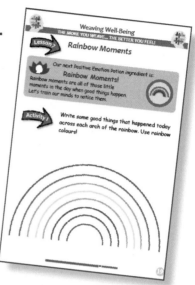

The **Weaving Well-Being** programme uses the approaches and methodologies as outlined in the SPHE guidelines (DES, 1999). The programme is comprised of ten specific lessons, which are designed to be ideally taught over consecutive weeks.

Each lesson consists of a PowerPoint introduction, suggested development ideas and two specific activities in the child's Activity Book. There is also a homework page consisting of an activity to be carried out over the week at home and reported back on.

The children gradually build a highly personal portfolio of work in their Activity Book, reflecting the unique components which enhance their individual well-being and resilience.

There is also a range of supplementary activities and photocopiable resources which can be used by the teacher to reinforce particular skills or strategies.

Active Learning

The lessons are designed to give the children an opportunity to be actively engaged in their own learning. They are encouraged to gather, record, interpret and analyse information about their thoughts, feelings and behaviours in an attempt to clarify the links between these processes. In doing so, they can become active agents in creating and maintaining their own well-being and mental health. This also encourages them to begin to take more responsibility and promotes action and decision making. Pair work is used to facilitate active learning throughout the lessons. Higher order thinking skills such as concluding, inferring and reflecting are also encouraged as part of the programme. The programme involves metacognition - children thinking about their own thinking.

Integration

Although the lessons are designed to be taught as specific SPHE lessons, plenty of scope is provided to integrate them across a wide variety of other curriculum areas. Literacy, visual arts, drama, music and SESE are among the subjects which lend themselves well to integration. This can help to embed the skills and concepts being taught while at the same time preventing further overcrowding of the curriculum.

ICT

There is scope when delivering this programme to incorporate the use of ICT resources. A number of links to appropriate websites have been included.

Strategies/Activities

The following strategies are used in the **Weaving Well-Being** programme, as they encourage active learning:

- talk and discussion

- drama

- responding through art

- checklists

- observing, recording and analysing

- critically evaluating

- mind maps

- responding through writing

- visual organisers

Child's artwork showing
one of the signs of well-being

Children's artwork showing
Gratitude Tree

Pages taken from
the accompanying
Positive Emotions
Pupil Activity Book

Part 1

All of the following short movies have been filmed on location in schools in Ireland and show children and teachers using and talking about various aspects of this *Weaving Well-Being* programme.

What is Positive Psychology?
by Fiona Forman (Co-Author) & Mick Rock (Co-Author) - Vimeo (2:50)
www.tinyurl.com/wwb-positive-psychology

What is Well-Being?
by Fiona Forman - Teacher and Co-Author - Vimeo (1:45)
www.tinyurl.com/wwb-wellbeing

Benefits of Enhancing Children's Well-Being
by Co-Authors Fiona Forman and Mick Rock - Vimeo (1:50)
www.tinyurl.com/wwb-enhancing

Enhancing Teacher Well-Being
by Co-Authors Fiona Forman and Mick Rock - Vimeo (2:23)
www.tinyurl.com/wwb-teacher

Research Project on Positive Psychology Interventions used in Schools
by Co-Authors Fiona Forman and Mick Rock - Vimeo (2:07)
www.tinyurl.com/wwb-research

Introduction to Co-Author Fiona Forman - Vimeo (4:36)
www.tinyurl.com/wwb-fiona

Introduction to Co-Author Mick Rock - Vimeo (2:38)
www.tinyurl.com/wwb-mick

Positive Emotions Programme - Classroom Scenes

Rainbow Moments - Vimeo (4:14)
www.tinyurl.com/wwb-rainbow

Random Acts of Kindness - Vimeo (1:36)
www.tinyurl.com/wwb-kindness

Feel-Good-Flow - Vimeo (2:04)
www.tinyurl.com/wwb-flow

Children's Views on Well-Being - Vimeo (2:05)
www.tinyurl.com/wwb-views

Language of Well-Being and Children's Self Assessment - Vimeo (5:02)
www.tinyurl.com/wwb-language

Additional movies available on the *Weaving Well-Being* Channel: www.vimeo.com/channels/wwb

Notes

Part 2:
Third Class Programme:
Positive Emotions

Background to Positive Emotions Programme

•

Specific Aims of the Positive Emotions Programme

•

Benefits of Positive Emotions

•

The Five Positive Emotions Ingredients

•

Structure of the Positive Emotions Programme

•

Background Information on the Psychological Concepts

•

Suggested Children's Literature

Background to Positive Emotions Programme

"Don't even start on your wellness routine unless there are positive emotions woven into it."
Barbara Fredrickson, President of International Positive Psychology Association

Research suggests that it is the frequency rather than the intensity of positive emotions which enhances well-being.[19] This means that experiencing many small moments of positive emotion regularly is more important to well-being than experiencing more intense moments every so often.

A growing body of research shows that positive emotions are linked to increased well-being across a number of areas. The Positive Psychology Professor Barbara Fredrickson identified these ten major positive emotions:

- joy
- gratitude
- serenity
- interest
- hope
- pride
- amusement
- inspiration
- awe
- love

Specific Aims of the Positive Emotions Programme

1. To introduce children to the concept of well-being.

2. To teach children that all emotions are normal and natural.

3. To help children to understand the importance of positive emotions to their well-being.

4. To allow the children to observe, discover and record the particular activities which generate positive emotions for them, in terms of an individual *Positive Emotion Potion.*

5. To give the children an opportunity to personalise their *Positive Emotion Potion* by deciding which ingredients give them most benefit and using more of them.

6. To encourage the children to use their *Positive Emotion Potion* every day to enhance their well-being.

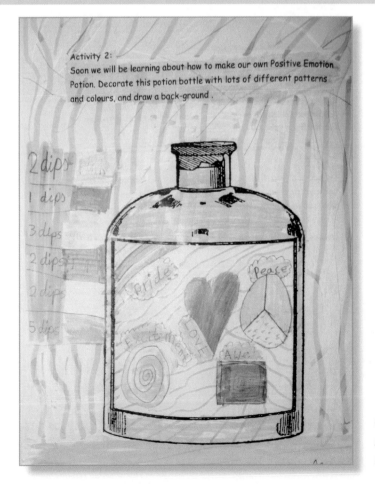

Child's artwork showing Positive Emotion Potion

Benefits of Positive Emotions

The experience of positive emotions can lead to a wide range of proven benefits.[6] The benefits of such genuinely felt emotions include:

- **Improved working memory.[14]**

- **Enhanced creative problem-solving.[15]**

- **Increased feelings of connection to others.[16]**

- **Greater resilience due to stress-buffering effects.[17]**

- **Better immune system functioning.[18]**

Page taken from the accompanying Positive Emotions Pupil Activity Book

The Five Positive Emotions Ingredients

In line with the research, showing that positive emotions are linked to increased well-being across a number of areas, this **Positive Emotions** programme introduces children to five evidence-based strategies to boost positive emotion on a daily basis. These strategies are:

1. **Attitude of Gratitude**
   Practising gratitude

2. **Feel-Good-Flow**
   Understanding and developing flow experiences

3. **Rainbow Moments**
   Counteracting the negativity bias

4. **Random Acts of Kindness**
   Performing acts of kindness

5. **Healthy Body - Happy Mind**
   Keeping physically healthy

Healthy Body + Happy Mind = Amazing Life!

The **Positive Emotions** programme introduces each of these strategies as ingredients which make up a **Positive Emotion Potion**. The children are given an opportunity to observe and record the effects of each strategy on their sense of well-being. After trying out all of the strategies on an individual basis, the children are then encouraged to put all of their 'ingredients' together and use their **Positive Emotion Potion** on a daily basis.

Structure of the Positive Emotions Programme

The **Positive Emotions** programme consists of ten lessons:

Lesson 1:
What is Well-Being?

Lesson 6:
Random Acts of Kindness

Lesson 2:
Positive Emotions

Lesson 7:
Rainbow Moments

Lesson 3:
Positive Emotion Potion

Lesson 8:
Healthy Body

Lesson 4:
Attitude of Gratitude

Lesson 9:
Positive Emotion Potion – Mix and Enjoy

Lesson 5:
Feel-Good-Flow

Lesson 10:
Review

It is recommended that the lessons are taught as one lesson per week.
This should be on consecutive weeks, if possible.

Page taken from the accompanying
Positive Emotions Pupil Activity Book

Background Information on the Psychological Concepts

Gratitude

Studies have shown that gratitude is associated with many positive outcomes such as greater happiness,[20] greater satisfaction with school, more optimism and fewer physical complaints.[21] Grateful people have been shown to be more pro-socially oriented in terms of being more forgiving, supportive and empathic.[22] Encouraging gratitude in children helps them to develop positive relationships and boost their mood.

Flow

Flow Theory, which was developed by Mihaly Csikszentmihalyi, relates to absorption in an activity which is challenging and satisfying. Skills are stretched to the limit in pursuit of a particular goal.[23]

Experience of flow activities is associated with enjoyment and mastery. Flow activities may be mental e.g. becoming engrossed in a stimulating book, or physical, e.g. engaging in a particular sport or creative activity. Teaching children about flow experiences and encouraging them to develop their talents through such activities may increase their enjoyment, mastery and well-being. Teachers can also try to provide experiences of flow in the learning environment, as this leads to greater learner engagement and concentration.[24] Suggestions for developing flow in the classroom are included in this lesson.

Kindness

The many benefits of kindness include an increased sense of accomplishment, confidence, optimism and usefulness. It can increase awareness of good fortune and provide a distraction from personal problems. Kindness also fosters cooperation and promotes positive social bonds.[25] Research has shown that to reap the benefits of kindness, choosing one day a week in which to perform at least five acts of kindness is associated with a greater increase in happiness than performing one act a day over the week. This experiment was conducted over a six week period.[26] Hence the **Random Acts of Kindness (R.A.K.)** lesson follows this structure. After the initial period the children can be encouraged to continue with their **R.A.K.** day themselves and discuss it from time to time.

Child's Artwork for Our Tree of Kindness

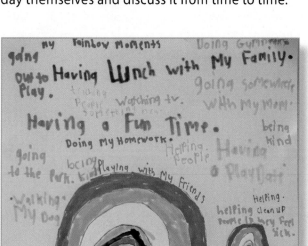

Children's artwork showing Rainbow Moments

Rainbow Moments

Rainbow Moments encourages the children to train their minds to focus on the many small positive events in their lives. It is based on Seligman's **Three-Good-Things** exercise.[27] This aims to counteract the negativity bias in which negative events or occurrences can dominate perception and affect mood.[28] Becoming more aware of positive events can balance out negative thinking and boost mood. As with the other interventions, after the initial period the children can be regularly encouraged to use and discuss **Rainbow Moments**.

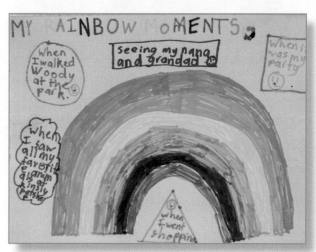

Healthy Body, Happy Mind

 Keeping fit, healthy and energetic reduces anxiety and stress, increases quality of life and reduces the risk of many diseases. Physical exercise can increase feelings of flow and self-mastery as well as boosting mood. Adequate sleep is required for optimal functioning and also for mood regulation.[29] Learning to cope with stress is also a vital component of well-being, as chronic exposure to overwhelming stress is linked to the development of depression.[30] Further strategies to deal with stress will be taught in other strands.

Child's poster showing one of the factors for a healthy body

The Value of Negative Emotions

Well-being does not involve feeling happy all the time, as experiencing and understanding a wide range of emotions is part of what makes us human and adds to the richness and complexity of life. The **Weaving Well-Being** programme teaches children that all emotions are important, natural and valuable. Negative emotions should be seen as valid information which may need to be acted on. For example, fear motivates individuals to avoid danger and anger may lead to action to solve problems or injustice.[31] Negative emotions should not be seen as bad or be suppressed, but rather as completely natural. Children can then be taught appropriate strategies for expressing and processing these emotions. This concept is developed more fully in the fourth class programme, **Tools of Resilience**.

Negative emotions can become detrimental to well-being however, if children become overwhelmed by them too frequently, or experience them too often in the absence of positive emotions to buffer against them. It can also be detrimental to well-being, if children frequently experience negative emotions of inappropriate onset, intensity or prolonged duration.

Balancing Negative and Positive Emotions

Research indicates that a ratio of around 3:1 of positive to negative emotions is necessary for individuals to thrive.[32] Children learn about this ratio in Lesson 2 of the programme. However, ratios of over 11:1 are counter-productive and can lead to a detachment from reality.

Suggested Children's Literature

The following books may be useful for teachers to use to support the embedding of the concepts taught through the programme. All have general themes of positive emotion.

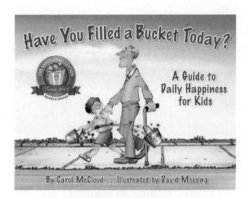

Have You Filled a Bucket Today?
by Carol McCloud

What Does it Mean to be Kind?
by Stephane Jorisch

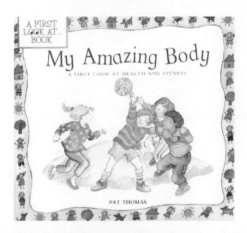

**A First Look At: Health and Fitness:
My Amazing Body**
by Pat Thomas

Happiness Is . . .
by Lisa Swerling and Ralph Lazar

The Giving Tree
by Shel Silverstein

**Did I Ever Tell You
How Lucky You Are?**
by Dr. Seuss

Thank You, World
by Alice B McGinty

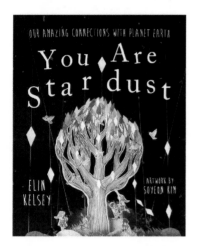

**You Are Stardust: Our Amazing
Connections With Planet Earth**
by Elin Kelsey

I Love My Amazing Body
by Jocelyn Scofield

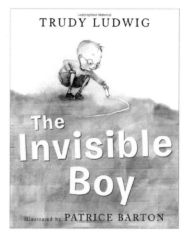

The Invisible Boy
by Trudy Ludwig

Ripple's Effect
by Shawn Achor and Amy Blankson

**Love Is My Favourite Thing:
A Plumdog Story**
by Emma Chichester Clark

An Awesome Book of Thanks!
by Dallas Clayton

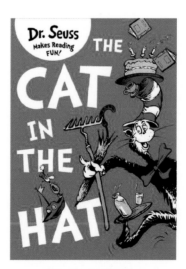

The Cat in the Hat
by Dr. Seuss

Notes

Part 3:
Lesson Plans & PowerPoint Slides

> **IMPORTANT: PLEASE READ THIS SHORT SECTION CAREFULLY BEFORE PROCEEDING TO THE LESSON PLANS.**

Introduction to Lesson Plans

The next section contains a lesson plan for each of the ten lessons of the *Positive Emotions* programme. Each lesson plan sets out the Strand and Strand Units of the SPHE curriculum that are covered by that lesson. It also includes the specific learning objectives for the children.

How each lesson should be developed is then briefly described. The information in this section will be similar for each lesson as the PowerPoint slides contain all the information needed to deliver the lesson. Most lessons include an introduction to each topic for the children followed by one or two activities and a homework assignment. The homework assignment is usually done over the course of a week. However, teachers should discuss how the children are getting on with it at various other times during the week. Any different approaches required for specific lessons will be highlighted in the "Development" section of the lesson plan.

PowerPoint Slides

PowerPoint slides are provided for each lesson. These slides are very comprehensive containing all the information required to deliver each session. Therefore, once the lesson plans have been reviewed, the **PowerPoint slides can be used to deliver the lesson.**

Cross-curricular links / Supplementary Activities

A number of cross-curricular links and supplementary activities have been included in this book. These contain additional information that can be used entirely at the discretion of each teacher. This section will be useful if a teacher would like to further embed the topic or integrate it with other subjects where appropriate.

Parent's Guide

A copy of the **Parent's Guide** is included at the back of this book (pages 70-73). This guide is presented as a 4 page pull-out in the children's Activity Book. It is designed to give parents a brief introduction to the **"Weaving Well-Being"** programme and to help them support their children as they complete the **Positive Emotions** programme.

Well-Being Self-Assessment Activity

Teachers can ask the children to fill this in to get a snap-shot at any given time of the children's perception of their own well-being. They can be encouraged to choose one of the indicators to work on over a period of time and self-evaluate their progress. Parental involvement in this process can be very valuable, so this can form part of the children's homework from time to time.

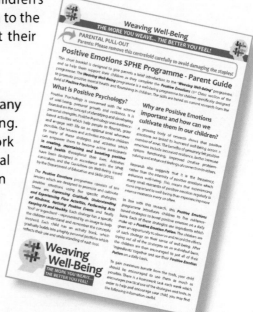

This can be found in the centre of the accompanying pupil's Positive Emotions Activity Book. A copy is also included in this Teacher Resource Book (pages 70-73).

Lesson 1: What is Well-Being?

SPHE Strand: *Myself*

Strand Units: Self-identity (Self-awareness & Developing self-confidence) / Taking care of my body (Health and well-being) / Growing and changing (Feelings and emotions).

The child should be enabled to:

- *explore factors that influence his/her self-image*
- *identify personal preferences, dreams for future and hopes*
- *express personal opinions, feelings, thoughts and ideas*
- *realise that each individual has some responsibility for his/her health*
- *talk about and reflect on a wide variety of feelings and emotions and the various situations where these may be experienced and how they may be expressed*
- *explore how feelings can influence one's life*

Objectives

1. To introduce the children to the concept of well-being.
2. To allow the children to discover which activities increase their well-being.

Development

- Show and discuss the PowerPoint slides.
- Discuss and complete one or both of the activities in the children's Activity Book.
- Discuss and set the homework page.

Cross-curricular links / Supplementary Activities

- Complete a 'Well-Being' acrostic poem using the Supplementary Worksheet - SW1(page 62).
- Think of the parts of well-being. Can you think of a movie or book character who shows high levels of well-being? Write a paragraph about them.
- *What is Wellbeing* - Co-author Fiona giving a teacher's overview of Well-being. - Vimeo (1:45)
  www.tinyurl.com/wwb-wellbeing
- Use the *'Well-being Snail Game'* for your class to work in groups on well-being.
  The resource is held on the Scottish Government Website and can be found at:
  www.tinyurl.com/wwb-snailgame
- Take part in an exercise break with fun exercises using one of the following YouTube movies:
  Blast Off - Fresh Start Fitness - Physical Workout - GoNoodle.com - YouTube (2:43)
  www.tinyurl.com/wwb-blastoff1
  I Get Loose - Koo Koo Kanga Roo - Physical Workout - GoNoodle.com - YouTube (1:33)
  www.tinyurl.com/wwb-getloose1
- Listen to some *'Zen Music for Wellbeing'* from Yellow Brick Cinema (YouTube) while practising relaxation in class using the *'Weather Massage'* from sense.org.uk
  Weather Massage: www.tinyurl.com/wwb-weathermassage
  Relaxing Music: www.tinyurl.com/wwb-zenmusic - YouTube (3:00:00)
- Whole School Approach: Set up a *'Nurture Room'* to support the emotional well-being of more vulnerable children - see: www.tinyurl.com/wwb-nurtureroom
- *Children's Views on Well-Being* - Vimeo (2:05)
  Listen to children in 4th class giving their views on the benefits of mindfulness.
  www.tinyurl.com/wwb-views

Lesson 1: PowerPoint Slides
What is Well-Being?

Lesson 1 PowerPoint is available digitally on the DVD accompanying this book.

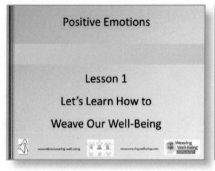

Lesson 2: Positive Emotions

SPHE Strand: *Myself*

Strand Units: Self-identity (Self-awareness & Developing self-confidence) / Taking care of my body (Health and well-being) / Growing and changing (Feelings and emotions)

The child should be enabled to:

- *explore factors that influence his/her self-image*

- *identify personal preferences, dreams and hopes for future*

- *express personal opinions, feelings, thoughts and ideas*

- *realise that each individual has some responsibility for his/her health*

- *talk about and reflect on a wide variety of feelings and emotions and the various situations where these may be experienced and how they may be expressed*

- *explore how feelings can influence one's life*

Objectives

1. That the children will understand that all emotions are normal and natural.

2. To introduce the children to the sub-group of emotions known as **Positive Emotions**.

3. To give the children the opportunity to discover and track their experiences of positive emotions.

4. To allow the children to observe, discover and record the particular activities which generate positive emotions for them.

5. To help the children to understand that three positive emotions are needed to balance one negative emotion.

Development

- Show and discuss the PowerPoint slides.

- Discuss and complete one or both of the activities in the children's Activity Book.

- Discuss and set the homework page.

Lesson 2: Cross-curricular Links / Supplementary Activities

- Design a word art poster on **Positive Emotions** using Supplementary Worksheet - SW2A (page 63).

- Complete the **Positive Emotions** crossword using Supplementary Worksheet - SW2B (page 64).

- Compile a class bar chart on the most frequently felt positive emotions, based on the **Positive Emotions** tracker homework sheets - pages 30-31 of the pupil's **Positive Emotions Activity Book**.

- Joke breaks. Allow the children to write down their two favourite jokes for homework. Collect the jokes and keep them in a container / jar. Pull out jokes at random times during the day for a joke break. Allow the child to read their joke out aloud if they wish.

- In pairs, brainstorm ways to boost class positive emotions.

- Art activity - Happy Memory. Ask the children to think of a memory which makes them feel happy and to draw a picture of it.

- Allow the children five free minutes at random times during the week, in which the children are free to move around, chat to their friends, read, draw, etc.

- Listen and watch the following song from KidsTV123 (YouTube) and ask children to write their own song.
  The Feelings Song - www.tinyurl.com/wwb-feelings-song (3:12)

- **Positive Emotions Word Art** - Ana de Armas y Villada - YouTube (1:40)
  www.tinyurl.com/wwb-emotionswordart

- Music Breaks. Select one of these GoNoodle videos from YouTube and join in - www.tinyurl.com/wwb-gonoodle

Additional movies available on the **Weaving Well-Being** Channel: www.vimeo.com/channels/wwb

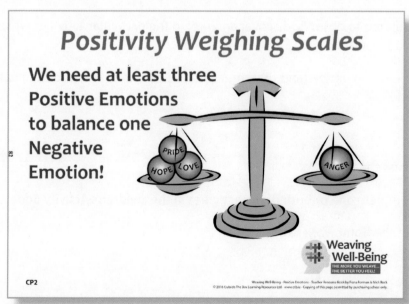

Class Poster (CP2) - Page 82

Lesson 2: PowerPoint Slides
Positive Emotions

 Lesson 2 PowerPoint is available digitally on the DVD accompanying this book.

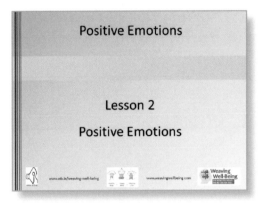

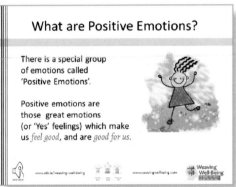

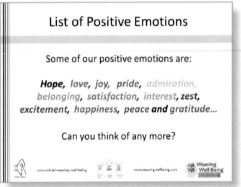

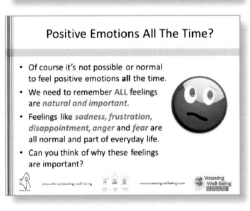

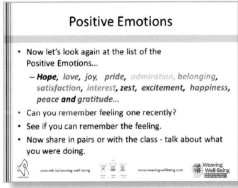

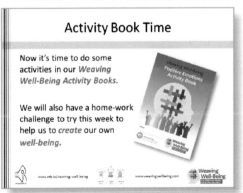

Lesson 3: Positive Emotion Potion

SPHE Strand: *Myself*

Strand Units: Self-identity (Self-awareness) / Taking care of my body (Health and well-being) / Growing and changing (As I grow I change & Feelings and emotions) / Making decisions

The child should be enabled to:

- *explore factors that influence his/her self-image*

- *identify personal preferences, dreams and hopes for future*

- *realise that each individual has some responsibility for his/her health and that this responsibility increases as he/she gets older*

- *recognise the emotional changes that have taken place since infancy*

- *explore how feelings can influence one's life*

- *explore and discuss that factors that influence personal decisions and choices and the different levels of thought involved in making a decision*

Objectives

1. That the children will understand the concept of a potion, i.e. separate ingredients coming together to make something which has a certain effect.

2. To encourage children to think about, observe and record the links between certain activities and the emotions they generate.

3. To allow the children to predict which types of activities might be needed to make a positive emotion potion.

Development

- Show and discuss the PowerPoint slides.

- Discuss and complete one or both of the activities in the children's Activity Book.

- Discuss and set the homework page.

Lesson 3: Cross-curricular Links / Supplementary Activities

 30+ Magical Harry Potter Inspired Crafts and Activities from One Crazy House
Art Construction: /Fabric and Fibre: Why not make a robe for Harry Potter / Hermione
or construct a wand for Ron in Hogwarts?
www.tinyurl.com/wwb-hpcrafts

 Creative Positive Emotions - *Thai Life Insurance* advert - *thaigoodstories.com* - YouTube (3:05)
www.tinyurl.com/wwb-ad-positiveemotions

 Harry Potter Potions Class Experiments from *imaginationsoup.net*.
Follow a Harry Potter Recipe to make a magic potion.
www.tinyurl.com/wwb-hpreceipe

 Poetry for Kids with Fun Activities from *pinterest.com*.
Write poems of different types (e.g. Cinquain, Haiku, Acrostic, etc.) about '***My Magic Potion***'.
www.tinyurl.com/wwb-writepoems

 Mad Scientist Potion Station from *pinterest.com*.
Select a Science experiment to complete.
www.tinyurl.com/wwb-se

 History of Magic from *themiddleages.net*.
Explore the history of magic during the middle ages.
www.tinyurl.com/wwb-historyofmagic

 Maths Magic Squares from
worksheetworks.com.
Create your own magic squares.
www.tinyurl.com/wwb-magicsquares

 Maths Magic & Tricks - Get children to think
creatively about Maths with '***Maths Magic to
amaze your friends***' using the links below:

> ***Is it Magic or is it Maths?*** from
> *NRICH (Enriching Mathematics)*
> www.tinyurl.com/wwb-mathsmagic1
> ***Math Magic / Number Fun / Maths Tricks***
> from *easycalculation.com*
> www.tinyurl.com/wwb-mathsmagic2
> ***MathSphere Maths Magic*** from
> *mathsphere.co.uk*
> (includes Clasroom Posters)
> www.tinyurl.com/wwb-mathsmagic3

Additional movies available on
the ***Weaving Well-Being*** Channel:
www.vimeo.com/channels/wwb

Class Poster (CP9) - Page 88

Lesson 3: PowerPoint Slides
Positive Emotion Potion

 Lesson 3 PowerPoint is available digitally on the DVD accompanying this book.

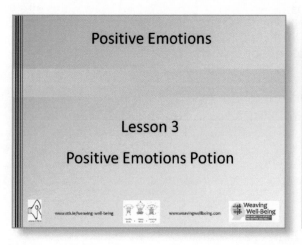

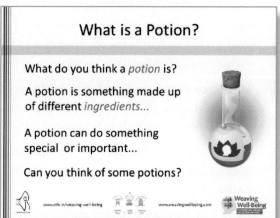

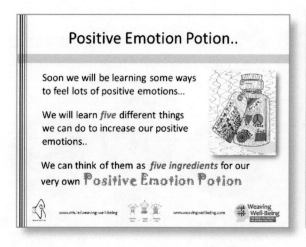

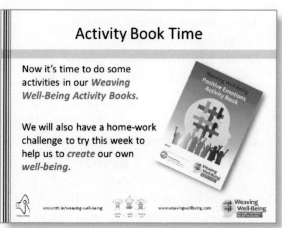

Lesson 4: Attitude of Gratitude

SPHE Strand: *Myself*

Strand Unit: Growing and changing (Feelings and emotions)

The child should be enabled to:

- *talk about and reflect on a wide variety of feelings and emotions and the various situations where these may be experienced and how they may be expressed*

- *identify strong feelings and learn how to express and cope with these feelings*

- *explore how feelings can influence one's life*

SPHE Strand: : *Myself and Others*

Strand Unit: Myself and my family / Relating to others

The child should be enabled to:

- *recognise and explore how language can be used to foster inclusiveness*

- *appreciate the need for and the importance of friendship and interacting with others*

Objectives

1. That the children will understand the effects of practising gratitude, on themselves and on others.
2. To allow the children an opportunity to practise gratitude and to observe and record the effect on their well-being.

Development

- Show and discuss PowerPoint slides.
- Discuss and complete one or both of the activities in the children's Activity Book.
- Discuss and set the homework page.

Lesson 4: Cross-curricular Links / Supplementary Activities

- Have a classroom **Gratitude Tree** display - the children write down things that they are grateful for on leaves and attach them to the tree using Supplementary Worksheet - SW4 (page 66).

- Make a classroom **Gratitude Collage**. Let the children cut out or draw pictures of things they are grateful for and put them together to make a colourful collage. Use photos too!

- Choose an item as a **Gratitude Object** (maybe a small toy or funny character.) Show it at random times during the week. When the children see it, they stop and have a silent moment while they remember some things they are thankful for. Let them aim for five, counting on their fingers.

- Let the children write and decorate a thank-you note to someone, then post or deliver it by hand.

- Make thank-you cards from the class to people who help them, e.g., the school care-taker, cleaners, lollipop lady, etc.

- Let the children design and make inspiring **Gratitude Posters** using well known quotes or their own slogans/quotes. Display them around the classroom and school.

- Encourage the children to keep a **Gratitude Journal** daily. Share your own entries also.

- Do a class brainstorm on things which we often take for granted.

- Challenge the children to try use gratitude when they are upset at the outcome of a particular situation. Acknowledge that this is not easy and praise any attempts. Ask them can they see any silver-lining and encourage them to work on this skill over time.

- Ask the children to write a story or poem called **"My Wonderful Life"** (if appropriate to individual needs).

- **Gratitude Kids** - Animation explaining *'Attitude of Gratitude'* for kids from *thelettersofgratitude.com* - YouTube (2:19)
  www.tinyurl.com/wwb-gratitudekids

  Additional movies available on the **Weaving Well-Being** Channel:
  www.vimeo.com/channels/wwb

Lesson 4: PowerPoint Slides
Attitude of Gratitude

Lesson 4 PowerPoint is available digitally on the DVD accompanying this book.

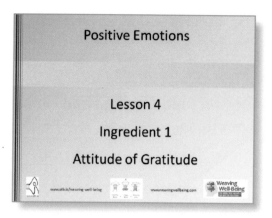

Positive Emotions

Lesson 4

Ingredient 1

Attitude of Gratitude

Our First Ingredient ...

The first ingredient in our *Positive Emotion Potion is....* *Attitude of Gratitude.*

Thank You!

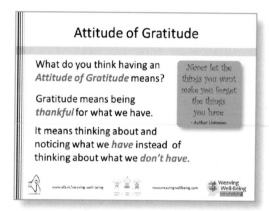

Attitude of Gratitude

What do you think having an *Attitude of Gratitude* means?

Gratitude means being *thankful* for what we have.

It means thinking about and noticing what we *have* instead of thinking about what we *don't have.*

Never let the things you want make you forget the things you have
- Author Unknown

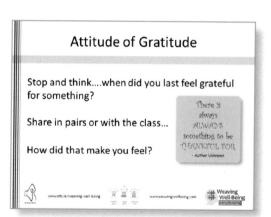

Attitude of Gratitude

Stop and think....when did you last feel grateful for something?

Share in pairs or with the class...

How did that make you feel?

There is always ALWAYS something to be THANKFUL FOR
- Author Unknown

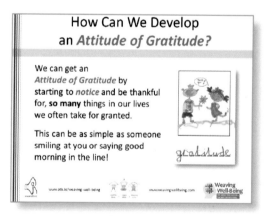

How Can We Develop an *Attitude of Gratitude?*

We can get an *Attitude of Gratitude* by starting to *notice* and be thankful for, **so many** things in our lives we often take for granted.

This can be as simple as someone smiling at you or saying good morning in the line!

gratitude

What are You Grateful for Today?

Now think about all the things you are grateful for today.....

Activity Book Time

Now it's time to do some activities in our *Weaving Well-Being Activity Books.*

We will also have a home-work challenge to try this week to help us to *create* our own *well-being.*

Lesson 5: Feel-Good-Flow

SPHE Strand: *Myself*

Strand Unit: Growing and changing (As I grow I change & Feelings and emotions)

The child should be enabled to:

- *realise that growing and changing are continuous throughout life*
- *identify the skills and abilities acquired and the interests and pursuits taken up in recent years*
- *identify strong feelings and learn how to express and cope with these feelings*
- *explore how feelings can influence one's life*

SPHE Strand: *Myself and others*

Strand Unit: My friends and other people

The child should be enabled to:

- *appreciate the need for, and the importance of, friendship and interacting with others.*

Objectives

1. To introduce the concept of flow to the children.
2. To allow the children to identify which particular activities give them a flow experience.
3. To give the children an opportunity to practise flow activities and to observe and record the impact on their well-being.

Development

- Show and discuss PowerPoint slides.
- Discuss and complete one or both of the activities in the children's book.
- Discuss and set the homework page.

Lesson 5: Cross-curricular Links / Supplementary Activities

- Have a class discussion on which activities in class they feel gives them flow, e.g. art, creative writing, maths drills, etc. Compile a list *'Our Flow Activities'*. Let the children make posters in pairs or groups about these activities. Try to incorporate as many flow activities into daily classroom practice as possible.

- Allow individual *'Feel-Good-Flow Time'* in which children choose one cognitive skill of their own choice to work on, e.g. handwriting, phonics, spelling, memorising, maths skills, etc. Allow five or ten minutes a few times weekly and see how it goes. Then give them some time to show or share how they have progressed with the rest of the class.

- Allow the children to brainstorm in pairs as to how to boost or increase *Feel-Good-Flow* activities in the class, then use *Think-Pair-Share*.

- Allow the children to Buddy-Up for challenging new topics. Explain to them that they have to challenge themselves to experience flow.

📹 *Flow - The Psychology of Optimal Experience* - Movie showing people in flow activities by *Shane Murphy* of *onitmedia.ie* - YouTube (9:45)
www.tinyurl.com/wwb-flowpsychology

The following short movie has been filmed on location in a Dublin school and shows children and teachers using and talking about aspects of the Weaving Well-Being programme.

📹 *Feel-Good-Flow* - Children talking about Feel-Good-Flow and what Flow means - Vimeo (2:04)
www.tinyurl.com/wwb-flow

Additional movies available on the
Weaving Well-Being Channel:
www.vimeo.com/channels/wwb

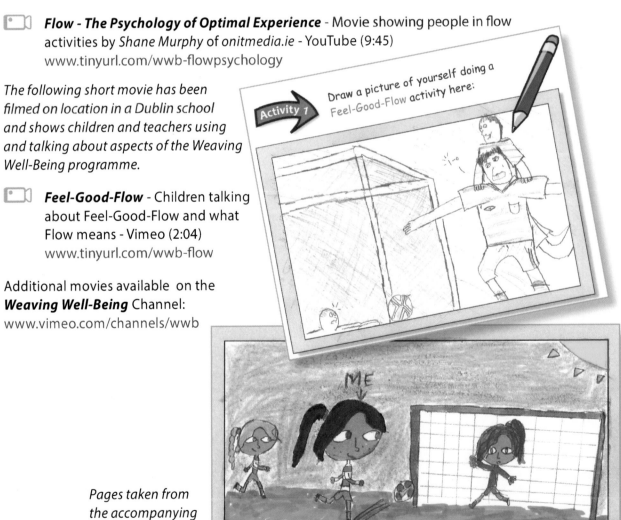

Pages taken from the accompanying Positive Emotions Pupil Activity Book

Lesson 5: PowerPoint Slides
Feel-Good-Flow

P🗔 Lesson 5 PowerPoint is available digitally on the DVD accompanying this book.

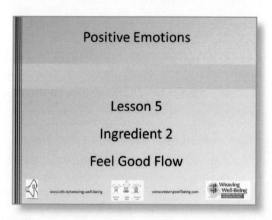

Positive Emotions

Lesson 5

Ingredient 2

Feel Good Flow

Our Second Ingredient

Now it's time for our second ingredient, it's called *Feel - Good - Flow.*

What do you think that is?

Feel - Good - Flow is when you get *totally involved and interested in what you are doing.*

You are *concentrating* and *you lose track of time.*

You are *developing a skill, and you feel proud of yourself afterwards.*

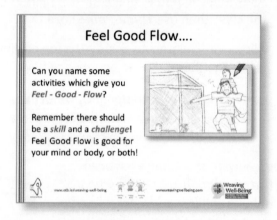

Feel Good Flow....

Can you name some activities which give you *Feel - Good - Flow*?

Remember there should be a *skill* and a *challenge*! Feel Good Flow is good for your mind or body, or both!

Feel Good Flow....

Some *Feel - Good - Flow* activities might be:

Sports, dancing, learning a musical instrument, painting, art and craft, reading, project work, learning something new, baking, writing stories or poems, memorizing something, working out puzzles or riddles..

Have a look!

- Let's watch a video of children talking about *Feel - Good - Flow* and how they use it. *(click image)*

Weaving Well-Being
THE MORE YOU WEAVE...
THE BETTER YOU FEEL!

Flow

Activity Book Time

Now it's time to do some activities in our *Weaving Well-Being Activity Books.*

We will also have a home-work challenge to try this week to help us to *create* our own *well-being.*

Lesson 6: Random Acts of Kindness (R.A.K.)

SPHE Strand: *Myself*

Strand Units: Self-identity (Self-awareness) / Taking care of my body (Health & well-being) / Growing and changing (As I grow I change & Feelings and emotions)

The child should be enabled to:

- recognise, describe and discuss individual personality traits, qualities, strengths, limitations interests and abilities

- realise that each person has a unique contribution to make to situations

- begin to develop strategies to cope with the various worries or difficulties that he or she may encounter

SPHE Strand: *Myself and others*

Strand Unit: My friends and other people / Relating to others

The child should be enabled to:

- appreciate the need for and the importance of friendship and interacting with others

- recognise and explore how language can be used to foster inclusiveness

Objectives

1. To give the children an opportunity to discover the effects of being kind on their well-being and positive emotions.

Development

- Show and discuss PowerPoint slides.

- Discuss and complete one or both of the activities in the children's Activity Book.

- Discuss and set the homework page.

Lesson 6: Cross-curricular Links / Supplementary Activities

● Create a **Tree of Kindness** classroom display using the Supplementary Worksheet - SW6 (page 67) template. The children decorate their own flowers by writing their names in the middle and five kind acts which they performed on the petals. They then stick their flowers onto the tree outline.

● Encourage children to be **Kindness Detectives** – notice others doing kind acts and report back to the class.

● Choose a small toy or item to be the class **Kindness Object**. When someone does something kind for someone else, they give them the object and then that child must Pass on the Kindness by doing something kind for someone else. See how many days it takes for the object to pass to everyone – have a daily show of hands to remind children who has already received it.

● Think about doing a **Random Act of Kindness** for the class every now and then when they least expect it – maybe taking an item off their daily homework or giving them all a small treat.

● Do group or individual projects called **The Power of Kindness** in which children research and present famous or everyday examples of kindness.

● Discuss the idea of being kind to yourself and how sometimes we can be very hard on ourselves. How can we be kinder to ourselves?

● Encourage the children to ask themselves the questions:
"How can I help others today?" at the start of the day and
"How did I help others today?" at the end of the day.

● Introduce the word empathy to the children and encourage them to stop and think regularly about how others might be feeling. Explain to them that understanding the feelings of others is a kind thing to do.

🎥 **White Stuff Kindness Offensive Official** - News item about a RAK initiative in London from *thekindnessoffensive.com* - YouTube (3:13)
www.tinyurl.com/wwb-raknews

The following short movie has been filmed on location in a Dublin school and shows children and teachers using and talking about aspects of the Weaving Well-Being programme.

🎥 **Random Acts of Kindness** - Children talking about Random Acts of Kindness they completed and the benefits achieved - Vimeo (1:36)
www.tinyurl.com/wwb-kindness

Additional movies available on the **Weaving Well-Being** Channel:
www.vimeo.com/channels/wwb

Part 3
Lesson Plans and PowerPoint Slides

Lesson 6: PowerPoint Slides
Random Acts of Kindness

Lesson 6 PowerPoint is available digitally on the DVD accompanying this book.

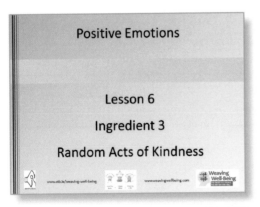

Positive Emotions

Lesson 6

Ingredient 3

Random Acts of Kindness

Our First Two Ingredients:

Can you remember the first two ingredients in our *Positive Emotion Potion?*
YES!! They are:
- *Attitude of Gratitude*
- *Feel - Good - Flow*

Lets talk about how you have been using them!

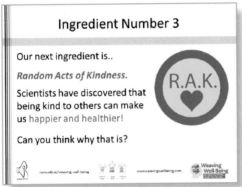

Ingredient Number 3

Our next ingredient is..
Random Acts of Kindness.
Scientists have discovered that being kind to others can make us happier and healthier!

Can you think why that is?

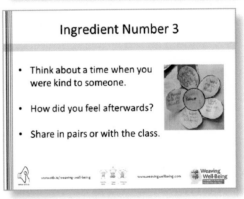

Ingredient Number 3

- Think about a time when you were kind to someone.
- How did you feel afterwards?
- Share in pairs or with the class.

*Kindness,
like a boomerang,
always returns.*

Think and talk about what you think this means.

Kindness

- Can you think of anybody who is well known for their kindness?
- It could be
  - character from a book
  - characters from a movie
  - a person in real life

Have a look!

- Let's watch a video of children talking about *Random Acts of Kindness* and how it made themselves and others feel. *(click image)*

Weaving Well-Being

Random Acts of Kindness

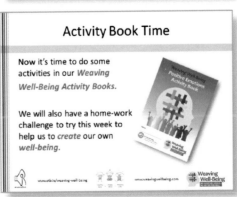

Activity Book Time

Now it's time to do some activities in our *Weaving Well-Being Activity Books.*

We will also have a home-work challenge to try this week to help us to *create* our own *well-being.*

Weaving Well-Being

47

© 2016 www.otb.ie

Part 3
Lesson Plans and PowerPoint Slides

Lesson 7: Rainbow Moments

SPHE Strand: *Myself*

Strand Units: Self-identity (Self-awareness) / Taking care of my body (Health & well-being) / Growing and changing (As I grow I change)

The child should be enabled to:

- *explore how feelings can influence one's life situations and friendships*

- *begin to develop strategies to cope with various worries and difficulties that he or she may encounter*

- *begin to appreciate the need for space and privacy in life*

SPHE Strand: *Myself and others*

Strand Unit: My friends and other people / Relating to others

The child should be enabled to:

- *appreciate the need for and the importance of friendship and interacting with others*

- *recognise and explore how language can be used to foster inclusiveness*

Objectives

1. That the children will start to notice all of the small positive things in their daily lives, to which they often do not attend.

2. To give the children the opportunity to notice and record these '*Rainbow Moments*' and to observe any positive emotions generated from them.

3. To help the children to understand that our minds are very good at noticing negative events and that we need to re-train them to notice positive events.

Development

- Show and discuss PowerPoint slides.

- Discuss and complete one or both of the activities in the children's Activity Book.

- Discuss and set the homework page.

Lesson 7: Cross-curricular Links / Supplementary Activities

- Encourage the children to use the *Rainbow Moments* activity in subsequent weeks by continuing to record their own *Rainbow Moments* in a notebook each morning or using Supplementary Worksheet - SW7 (page 68). This can provide a positive start to their day.

- Creative writing- *The End of the Rainbow*

- Ask the children to discuss which particular positive emotion each *Rainbow Moment* gives them.

- *Feelings and Colours Song* - Listen and watch this song discussing the colour of each emotion. Children create and perform their own *'Look at me'* song in pairs or in groups outlining the colours of their emotions – from *thekindnessoffensive.com* - YouTube (2:42) www.tinyurl.com/wwb-emotioncolours

- *Fun Weather Facts for Kids* - Check out the fun rainbow facts for kids and enjoy a range of interesting information about rainbows - from *sciencekids.co.nz* www.tinyurl.com/wwb-rainbowfacts

- *How do Rainbows Form?* - Use this link for a Science (Light) activity to learn how rainbows are formed - from *discoverykids.com* www.tinyurl.com/wwb-formingrainbows

- *How is a Rainbow Formed?* - Science Experiment: Making a Rainbow - from *Japinder Kaur* - YouTube (3:44) www.tinyurl.com/wwb-rainbowexperiment

- *Rainbow Art Themes* - Mixing primary and secondary colours to make a colour wheel - from *color-wheel-artist.com* www.tinyurl.com/wwb-rainbowart

The following short movie has been filmed on location in a Dublin school and shows children and teachers using and talking about aspects of the Weaving Well-Being programme.

- *Rainbow Moments* - Explanation of Rainbow Moments with lots of children's examples and children talking about why they like them - Vimeo (4:14) www.tinyurl.com/wwb-rainbow

Additional movies available on the **Weaving Well-Being** Channel: www.vimeo.com/channels/wwb

Page taken from the accompanying Positive Emotions Pupil Activity Book

Lesson 7: PowerPoint Slides
Rainbow Moments

Lesson 7 PowerPoint is available digitally on the DVD accompanying this book.

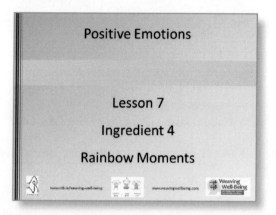

Positive Emotions

Lesson 7

Ingredient 4

Rainbow Moments

Our Next Ingredient....

- Can you remember our first three ingredients?
- Let's talk about how you have been using them.
- It's now time to learn about our next ingredient:

  Rainbow Moments!

What are Rainbow Moments?

Rainbow Moments are all of those lovely little moments during the day when things go well for us. Can you think of any examples?

You play a fun game at break, you watch a great movie, you spend time with your friend, you notice something beautiful, someone is kind or helpful to you, you feel proud of yourself for finishing something difficult...

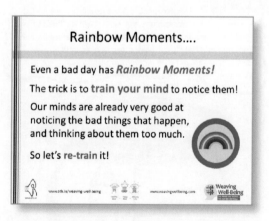

Rainbow Moments....

Even a bad day has *Rainbow Moments!*

The trick is to **train your mind** to notice them!

Our minds are already very good at noticing the bad things that happen, and thinking about them too much.

So let's **re-train** it!

Let's Notice our Rainbow Moments..

Your challenge this week is to re-train your mind so that it starts to notice your *Rainbow Moments!*

Let's try to notice three each day and write them down. Good Luck and enjoy your challenge!

Have a look!

- Let's watch a video of children talking about their own *Rainbow Moments* and how they make them feel. *(click image)*

Weaving Well-Being
THE MORE YOU WEAVE... THE BETTER YOU FEEL!

Rainbow Moments

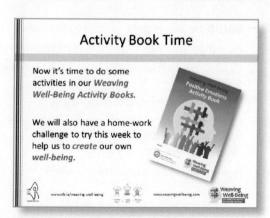

Activity Book Time

Now it's time to do some activities in our *Weaving Well-Being Activity Books.*

We will also have a home-work challenge to try this week to help us to *create* our own *well-being.*

Lesson 8: Healthy Body, Happy Mind

SPHE Strand: *Myself*

Strand Units: Self-identity (Self-awareness) / Taking care of my body (Health & well-being) / Growing and changing (As I grow I change)

The child should be enabled to:

- *identify realistic personal goals and targets and how these can be achieved in the short or long term*

- *understand and appreciate what it means to be healthy and to have a balanced life-style*

- *realise that each individual has some responsibility for his/her health and that this responsibility increases as he/she gets older*

- *identify the skills and abilities acquired and the interests and pursuits taken up in recent years*

Objectives

1. That the children will understand three key steps to keeping their bodies healthy.

2. That the children will begin to explore the links between keeping their bodies healthy and their well-being.

3. To give the children the opportunity to implement these three steps and to observe and record the effect on their well-being and positive emotions.

Development

- Show and discuss PowerPoint slides.

- Discuss and complete one or both of the activities in the children's Activity Book.

- Discuss and set the homework page.

Lesson 8: Cross-curricular Links / Supplementary Activities

- Visual art: make a collage of a healthy meal on a paper plate.

- Think-Pair-Share : Ten ways to get one hour of exercise daily.

[ICT] *My Plate Nutrition Learning Activity* - Design healthy daily menus - from *nourishinteractive.com*
www.tinyurl.com/wwb-printnutrition

[ICT] *Talking My Plate* - Interactive Healthy Food Game: Listen to the Talking Plate explain about portion sizes and parts of a healthy diet e.g. carbohydrates, proteins, etc. - from *nourishinteractive.com*
www.tinyurl.com/wwb-plate

[video] *Dinostomp* - Dance-A-Long Video - Allow movement and exercise breaks regularly throughout the day by *Koo Koo Kanga Roo* - YouTube (3:37)
www.tinyurl.com/wwb-dinostomp

[ICT] *Sleep for Kids - Teaching kids the importance of Sleep* - Science: Read about the effects of sleep deprivation, brainstorm tips for getting a good night's sleep and encourage children to observe how they feel when they don't get enough sleep - from *sleepforkids.org*
www.tinyurl.com/wwb-sleepforkids

[video] *Why Do We Sleep?* - Animation explaining what happens while we sleep and the importance of sleep from *hooplakidz.com* - YouTube (2:00)
www.tinyurl.com/wwb-whysleep

[ICT] *Me and My Amazing Body* - A Read Aloud Activity Book by *Ali Scott*
www.tinyurl.com/wwb-myamazingbody

Additional movies available on the *Weaving Well-Being* Channel:
www.vimeo.com/channels/wwb

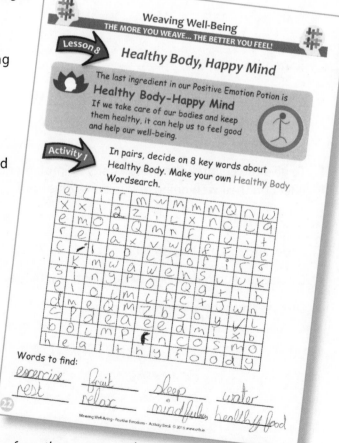

Page taken from the accompanying Positive Emotions Pupil Activity Book

Lesson 8: PowerPoint Slides
Healthy Body, Happy Mind

Lesson 8 PowerPoint is available digitally on the DVD accompanying this book.

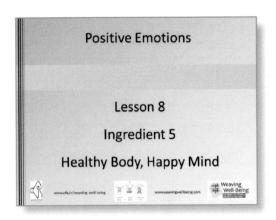

Positive Emotions

Lesson 8

Ingredient 5

Healthy Body, Happy Mind

Our First Four Ingredients....

Can you remember the first four ingredients of our *Positive Emotion Potion*?

Let's talk about them..
1. Attitude of Gratitude
2. Feel - Good - Flow
3. R.A.K.
4. Rainbow Moments

Which has been your favourite? Why?

Our Last Ingredient....

Our last ingredient is..
Healthy Body, Happy Mind!

- If we keep our bodies healthy, that helps our minds to stay healthy too. Why do you think that is?
- Can you think of ways for us to keep our bodies healthy?

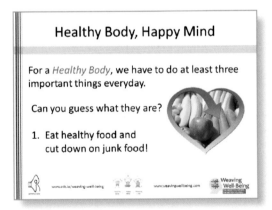

Healthy Body, Happy Mind

For a *Healthy Body*, we have to do at least three important things everyday.

Can you guess what they are?

1. Eat healthy food and cut down on junk food!

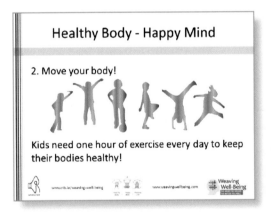

Healthy Body - Happy Mind

2. Move your body!

Kids need one hour of exercise every day to keep their bodies healthy!

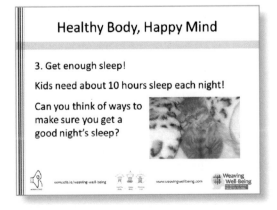

Healthy Body, Happy Mind

3. Get enough sleep!

Kids need about 10 hours sleep each night!

Can you think of ways to make sure you get a good night's sleep?

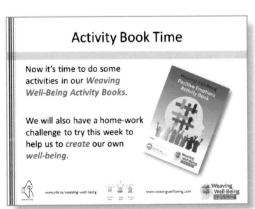

Activity Book Time

Now it's time to do some activities in our *Weaving Well-Being Activity Books*.

We will also have a home-work challenge to try this week to help us to *create* our own *well-being*.

Lesson 9: Positive Emotion Potion – Mix and Enjoy

SPHE Strand: *Myself*

Strand Units: Self-identity (Developing self-confidence) / Making decisions

The child should be enabled to:

- *become more confident in coping with change and with situations that are unfamiliar*

- *become aware of and think about choices and decisions that he/she makes every day*

- *explore and discuss the factors that influence personal decisions and choices and the different levels of thought involved in making a decision*

- *learn and begin to devise a simple decision-making strategy*

Objectives

1. To recap on all of the **Positive Emotion Potion** ingredients.

2. To enable the children to categorise particular activities into the correct type of ingredient.

3. To give the children an opportunity to practise using all of their ingredients and to observe and record the effects on their well-being and positive emotions.

4. To allow the children to individualise their potion ingredient amounts.

Development

- Show and discuss PowerPoint slides.

- Discuss and complete one or both of the activities in the children's Activity Book.

- Discuss and set the homework page.

Cross-curricular Links / Supplementary Activities

- Visual Art: Make Positive Emotions Posters and display them around the classroom.

- Make **Positive Emotion Potion** bookmarks so that children have a daily reminder of their five ingredients.

- Allow the children to look back on their list of activities which they compiled in Lesson 2. Do they have another personal / individual **Positive Emotion Potion** ingredient which hasn't been covered?

- Brainstorm ways to ensure **Positive Emotion Potion** ingredients are remembered and used.

- If a child seems stuck in a low or negative mood for no particular reason, ask them if they would like to select a particular **Positive Emotion Potion** ingredient to try out to see if it helps.

- Brainstorm a list of **Positive Emotion Potion** songs and play them regularly.

Lesson 9: PowerPoint Slides
Positive Emotion Potion –
Mix and Enjoy

 Lesson 9 PowerPoint is available digitally on the DVD accompanying this book.

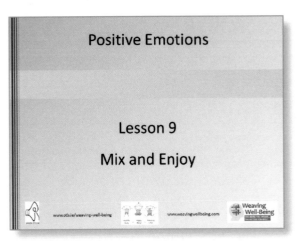

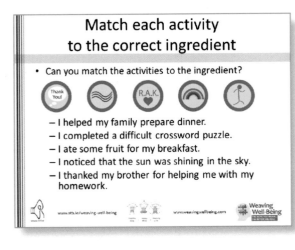

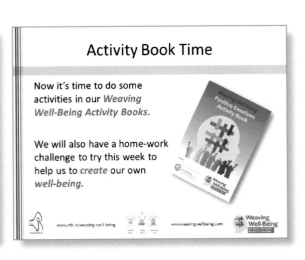

Lesson 10: Review

SPHE Strand: *Myself*

Strand Unit: Making decisions

The child should be enabled to:

- *become aware of and think about choices and decisions that he/she makes every day*

- *explore and discuss the factors that influence personal decisions and choices and the different levels of thought involved in making a decision*

- *learn and begin to devise a simple decision-making strategy*

- *recognise that opportunities to exercise choice can increase as responsibilities are accepted*

Objectives

1. To give the children an opportunity to personalise their **Positive Emotion Potion** by deciding how which ingredients give them most benefit and using more of them.

2. To encourage the children to use their **Positive Emotion Potion** every day to help their well-being.

Development

- Show and discuss PowerPoint slides.

- Discuss and complete one or both of the activities in the children's Activity Book.

- Discuss and set the homework page.

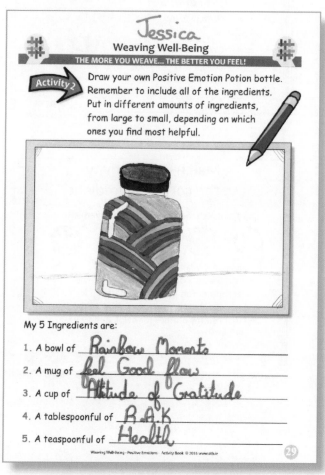

Page taken from the accompanying Positive Emotions Pupil Activity Book

Lesson 10: PowerPoint Slides Review

 Lesson 10 PowerPoint is available digitally on the DVD accompanying this book.

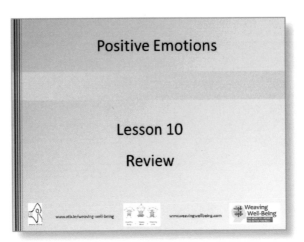

Positive Emotions

Lesson 10

Review

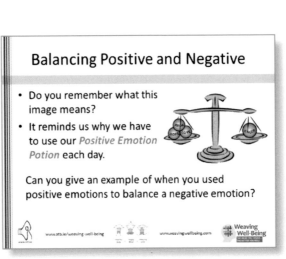

Looking Back at Mix and Enjoy

You've used your *Positive Emotion Potion* and selected your favourite Ingredient.

What was your favourite and why?

Balancing Positive and Negative

- Do you remember what this image means?
- It reminds us why we have to use our *Positive Emotion Potion* each day.

Can you give an example of when you used positive emotions to balance a negative emotion?

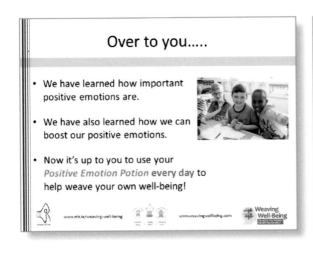

Over to you.....

- We have learned how important positive emotions are.

- We have also learned how we can boost our positive emotions.

- Now it's up to you to use your *Positive Emotion Potion* every day to help weave your own well-being!

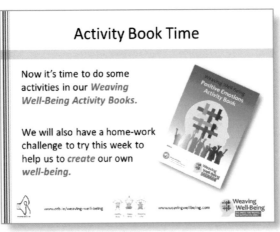

Activity Book Time

Now it's time to do some activities in our *Weaving Well-Being Activity Books*.

We will also have a home-work challenge to try this week to help us to *create* our own *well-being*.

Notes

Part 4:
Supplementary Materials

All materials in this section are available on the accompanying DVD

Supplementary Worksheets

•

Well-Being Self-Assessment Check up

•

Parental Guide

•

Class Posters

•

References

Notes

Supplementary Worksheets (SW)

Lesson 1: What is Well-Being?

Well-Being Acrostic Poem - SW1 (page 62)
Brainstorm well-being words on the board to recall Lesson 1 information introduced to the children. They can then work individually, in pairs or in groups to create their own well-being acrostic poem.

Lesson 2: Positive Emotions

Positive Emotions word art template - SW2A (page 63)
Children can fill in the face with positive emotions words.

Positive Emotions Crossword - SW2B (page 64)
Use the clues to complete the crosswords.

Lesson 4: Attitude of Gratitude

Blank leaves for class Gratitude Tree Display - SW4 (page 66)
Give out the blank leaf templates to create a Gratitude Tree Display and allow children to write down things for which they are grateful.

Lesson 6: Random Acts of Kindness

Tree of Kindness Flower - SW6 (page 67)
Distribute the *Tree of Kindness* flower templates to create a class display. Get the children to write their name in the middle of the flower. Then write a *Random Act of Kindness* they did on each of the petals. They then stick their flowers on a tree outline.

Lesson 7: Rainbow Moments

My Rainbow Moments - SW7 (page 68)
Use this template to encourage the children to continue to record their *Rainbow Moments* on subsequent weeks.

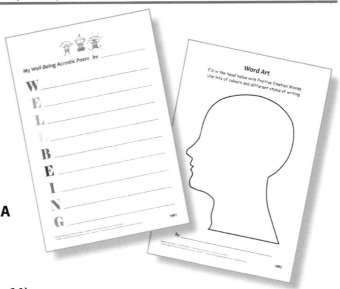
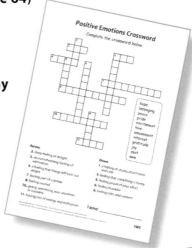
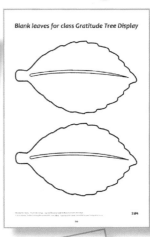

My Well-Being Acrostic Poem   by _____

W _____

E _____

L _____

L _____

B _____

E _____

I _____

N _____

G _____

Word Art

Fill in the head below with Positive Emotion Words.
Use lots of colours and different styles of writing.

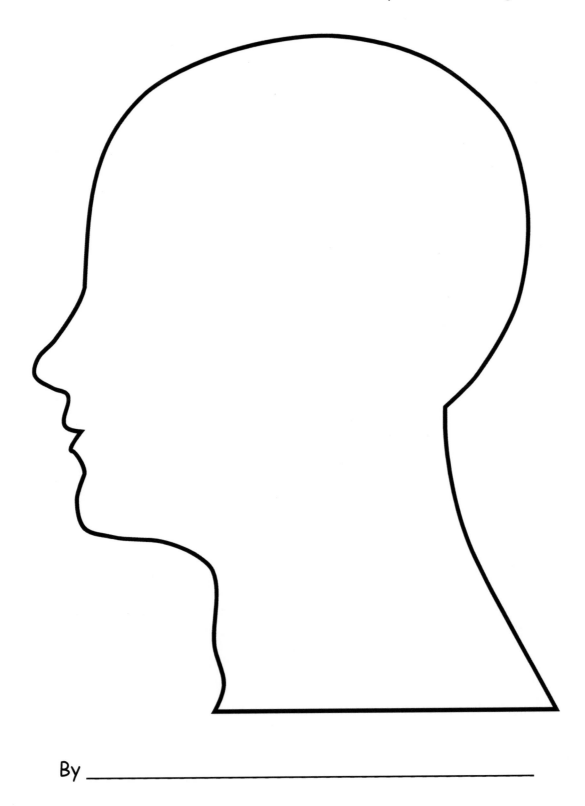

By _____

Positive Emotions Crossword

Complete the crossword below

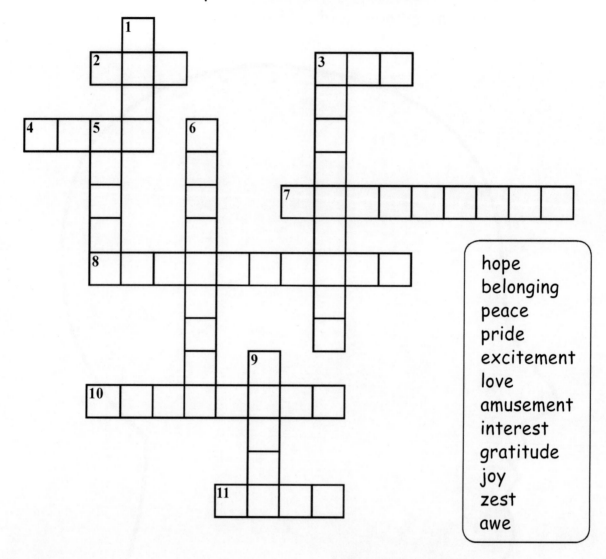

hope
belonging
peace
pride
excitement
love
amusement
interest
gratitude
joy
zest
awe

Across

2. deep feeling of delight

3. an overwhelming feeling of admiration

4. a feeling that things will turn out alright

7. feeling part of a group

8. feeling excited

10. giving something your attention or curiosity

11. having lots of energy and enthusiam

Down

1. a feeling of strong attachment and care

3. feeling that something is funny

5. feeling proud of your effort

6. feeling thankful

9. feeling calm and content

Name: _____

Weaving Well-Being - Positive Emotions - Teacher Resource Book by Fiona Forman & Mick Rock
© 2016 Outside The Box Learning Resources Ltd - www.otb.ie - Copying of this page permitted by purchasing school only.

SW2B

Positive Emotions Crossword
Solution

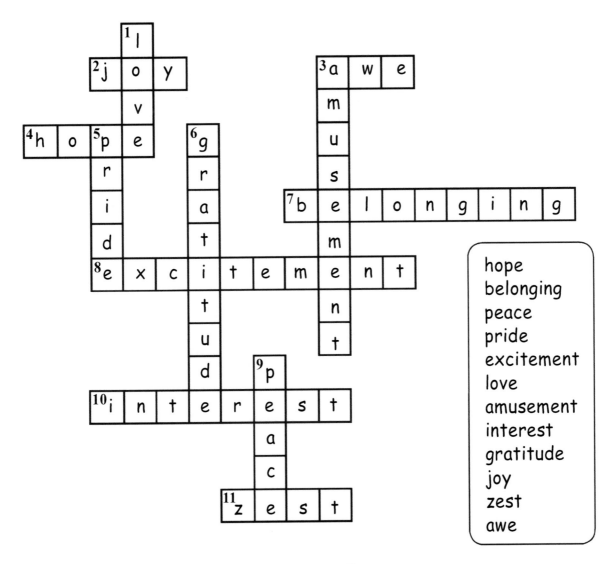

hope
belonging
peace
pride
excitement
love
amusement
interest
gratitude
joy
zest
awe

Across

2. deep feeling of delight
3. an overwhelming feeling of admiration
4. a feeling that things will turn out alright
7. feeling part of a group
8. feeling excited
10. giving something your attention or curiosity
11. having lots of energy and enthusiam

Down

1. a feeling of strong attachment and care
3. feeling that something is funny
5. feeling proud of your effort
6. feeling thankful
9. feeling calm and content

Name: _____

Weaving Well-Being - Positive Emotions - Teacher Resource Book by Fiona Forman & Mick Rock

SW2B

Blank leaves for class Gratitude Tree Display

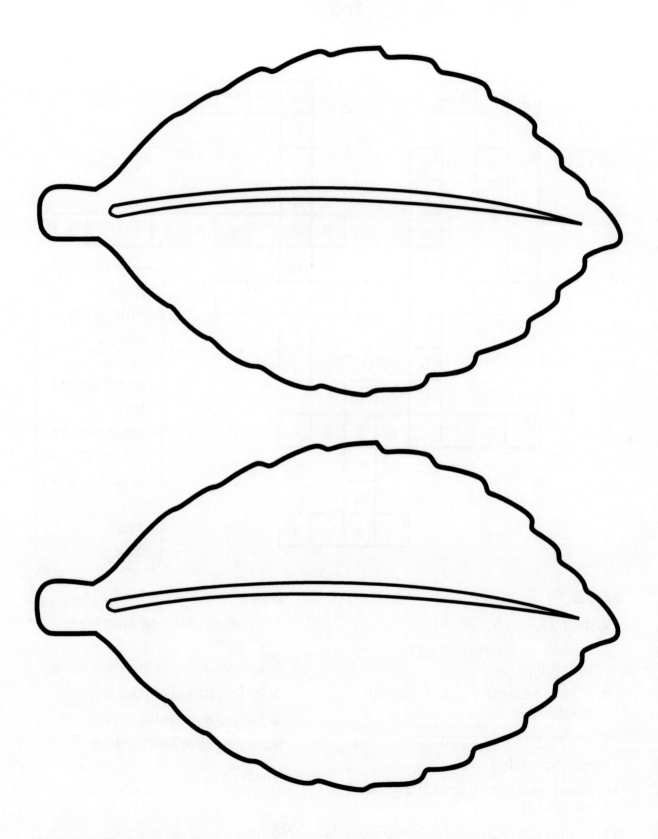

SW4

Tree of Kindness

Write your name in the middle of the flower, then write
a random act of kindness you did on each of the petals.
Decorate the flower with pictures and patterns.

Rainbow Moments

Our minds are very good at noticing and remembering negative or bad things that happen to us. This can lead to negative moods which can last a long time!

Noticing our Rainbow Moments each day helps us to re-train our minds to notice all the little positive things which happen each day. Scientists have found out this can really help our moods.

My Rainbow Moments

MONDAY	1.	
	2.	
	3.	
TUESDAY	1.	
	2.	
	3.	
WEDNESDAY	1.	
	2.	
	3.	
THURSDAY	1.	
	2.	
	3.	
FRIDAY	1.	
	2.	
	3.	

Weaving Well-Being
THE MORE YOU WEAVE... THE BETTER YOU FEEL!

Well-Being Self-Assessment Check up

These Weaving Well-Being lessons have been designed to help you to notice and improve your well-being. Your teacher may ask you to fill it in from time to time to help you keep track of your own well-being. If you need help in a certain area, think of ways to improve on it and see if they work. Don't forget to ask your parents, friends and family for help, support and advice! Enjoy weaving your well-being!

😊 = I'm doing well in this area

😐 = I'm doing okay, room for improvement

☹ = I am not doing well and may need support or help in this area

Well-Being Signs	Date	Date	Date	Date	Date	Date	Date
I feel like I have plenty of energy to do the things I want or need to do.							
I feel like I get along with others most of the time.							
I know and use my strengths often.							
I regularly feel grateful for many things in my life.							
I feel that I have ways to cope with disappointments and problems.							
I often feel proud of myself for doing my best.							
I often help others.							
I can accept that I am OK just as I am.							

Weaving Well-Being - Positive Emotions - Teacher Resource Book by Fiona Forman & Mick Rock
© 2016 Outside The Box Learning Resources Ltd - www.otb.ie - Copying of this page permitted by purchasing school only.

SW8

Weaving Well-Being
THE MORE YOU WEAVE... THE BETTER YOU FEEL!

PARENTAL PULL-OUT
Parents: Please remove this centrefold carefully to avoid damaging the staples!

Positive Emotions SPHE Programme - Parent Guide

This short booklet is designed to give parents a brief introduction to the "*Weaving Well-Being*" programme and to help them support their children as they complete the *Positive Emotions* (3ʳᵈ Class) section of the programme. The *Weaving Well-Being* programme is a well-being programme for children specifically designed to promote positive mental health and flourishing in children. The skills are based on current research from the field of *Positive Psychology.*

What is Positive Psychology?

Positive Psychology is concerned with the science of well-being, personal growth and resilience. It is founded on the concept of identifying and developing personal strengths. Positive Psychology uses evidence-based activities which help people to flourish, grow and engage with life on an optimal level whenever possible. Our lessons and activities introduce children to many of these strategies and activities which can empower them to become active participants **in creating, maintaining and boosting positive mental health** throughout their lives. Activities have been designed in accordance with the SPHE curriculum, and the Guidelines on Well-Being issued by the Department of Education and Skills (2015).

The *Positive Emotions* programme consists of ten lessons which are designed to promote and cultivate positive emotions using five specific strategies. These are: *Expressing Gratitude, Understanding and Experiencing Flow Activities, Performing Acts of Kindness, Noticing Positive Events* and finally *Keeping Fit and Healthy*. Each strategy has a specific 'tool' or 'ingredient' - represented by an image to help the children understand and remember the concepts involved. Each child has an Activity Book, which gradually builds into a highly personal portfolio which reflects their use and understanding of each tool.

Why are Positive Emotions important and how can we cultivate them in our children?

A growing body of research shows that positive emotions are linked to increased well-being across a number of areas. The benefits of genuinely felt positive emotions include increased resilience, better immune system functioning, improved creative problem-solving and enhanced feelings of connection to others.

Research also suggests that it is the frequency, rather than the intensity of positive emotions which enhances well-being. This means that experiencing many small moments of positive emotion regularly is more important to well-being than experiencing more intense moments every so often.

In line with this research, this *Positive Emotions* programme introduces children to five evidence-based strategies through the lesson plans to boost positive emotion on a daily basis. Each of these strategies uses ingredients which make up a *Positive Emotion Potion*. The children are given an opportunity to observe and record the effects of each strategy on their sense of well-being. After trying out all of the strategies on an individual basis, the children are then encouraged to put all of their 'ingredients' together and use their *Positive Emotion Potion* on a daily basis.

To gain maximum benefit from the tools, your child should be encouraged to use them as much as possible. There is a homework task each week which encourages practical use of the strategies and tools. In order to help and encourage your child, you may find the following information useful.

Weaving Well-Being
THE MORE YOU WEAVE... THE BETTER YOU FEEL!

Lesson 1: What is Well-Being?

In this lesson, children discuss and learn what well-being means and the implications of taking care of our well-being in our daily lives. Children learn that well-being is linked with feeling good in both our body and mind and it allows us to cope with little problems, enjoy life and accept ourselves just as we are. Other benefits of caring for our well-being are discussed in terms of friendships and feeling connected with others, having energy and being proud of our efforts. Children are encouraged to try to remember a time when they felt any of these signs of taking care of their well-being and reconnect with that feeling.

How to support your child: Talk to your child about the importance of taking care of their well-being. Discuss why your child selected particular well-being words in their Activity Book and what it means to them. Give examples of your own understanding of well-being words and link situations in your life to times when you took care of your own well-being. Discuss how you can care for or enhance your well-being as a family.

Lesson 2: Positive Emotions

In this lesson children discuss that all emotions or feelings are normal, natural and important. A special group of emotions called *Positive Emotions* are discussed. Understanding that it is not possible to have positive emotions all the time is examined, but children learn that having plenty of positive emotions every day can help our well-being. Scientific research showing that we should have three positive emotions to balance one negative emotion is explored.

How to support your child: Encourage your child to explain when they have felt any of the positive emotions outlined in their *Positive Emotions Activity Book*. Give examples of times when you recall feeling any, or all of these positive emotions too. Reinforce that it is not possible to have positive emotions all the time and that all feelings, positive and negative, are normal and natural. Discuss the *Positive Emotion Tracker* in their Activity Book each night with your child, encouraging him/her to link the positive emotion to the activity that caused that emotion.

Lesson 3: Positive Emotion Potion

In this lesson, children are introduced to the idea that there are five special activities which can boost our positive emotions. These five activities are the ingredients in a *Positive Emotion Potion*. The meaning of a potion is discussed and children are encouraged to represent how they visualise their own *Positive Emotion Potion* in art form. The positive emotions experienced in the previous week's tracker are explored and children link their favourite positive emotion to the activity completed that week.

How to support your child: Discuss the meaning of each of the positive emotions in this week's homework (*Pride, Interest, Belonging, Excitement, Amusement, Awe, Zest, Peace, Love and Gratitude*). Give examples of what might give rise to this emotion for you. Encourage your child to choose one positive emotion which is meaningful to him/her and discuss activities that will help your child feel this emotion. Discuss the benefits for your child of feeling that emotion.

Weaving Well-Being
THE MORE YOU WEAVE... THE BETTER YOU FEEL!

Lesson 4: Ingredient 1: Attitude of Gratitude

Children are introduced to the first ingredient of the **Positive Emotion Potion - Attitude of Gratitude**. Gratitude is explained as feeling thankful for, and noticing what we have, rather than what we don't have. Children are encouraged to think about things they are lucky to have. These are recalled in terms of family, friends, home, toys, schools, pets, etc. Children think of someone in their lives who they would particularly like to thank. A plan for a Gratitude Letter is discussed and prepared. For homework your child will be writing a Gratitude Letter. Ask your child if they need any help or support with this, being mindful that the letter may be for you!

How to support your child: Discuss what an **Attitude of Gratitude** means to your child. Reinforce this concept by highlighting key things in your life for which you are thankful. These things can be as simple as noticing how someone asked you how you are, smiled at you during the day or offered assistance in some way. Remember that *'Gratitude is the best Attitude'* and there is always something to be thankful for in our day.

Lesson 5: Ingredient 2: Feel-Good-Flow

Ingredient 2 of the **Positive Emotion Potion** is explained and explored. It is identified as **Feel-Good-Flow** and is explained as getting totally involved and interested in what you are doing, concentrating on the activity and losing track of time. In this process you are enhancing your skills, or learning a new skill and feeling proud of yourself. Children identify **Flow** activities they experience both in school and in their home life. They are encouraged to participate in more of these activities and reminded that this is the second ingredient in improving their well-being through our **Positive Emotion Potion.**

How to support your child: Discuss your child's **Feel-Good-Flow** activity in their Activity Book, identifying why they selected this activity. To help your child to reinforce the concept of **Feel-Good-Flow,** explore what the challenge was in the activity, the resulting skill acquired and the emotion created. For homework this week, encourage your child to practise their **Flow** activity for thirty minutes each day. Link your own **Feel-Good-Flow** activities to your child's, reminding your child that these activities are different for each individual and are a life-long practice to maintain and enhance our well-being.

Lesson 6: Ingredient 3: Random Acts of Kindness (R.A.K.)

The many benefits of kindness are explored in Ingredient 3 of the **Positive Emotion Potion - Random Acts of Kindness (R.A.K.)**. It is explained to children that being kind to others has a physical reaction on our bodies and makes us happier and healthier. Children discuss times when they acted in a kind manner towards another person or when someone was kind to them. This act is linked to the emotion created as a result. Traits of kind characters in children's literature are explored and children discuss kind acts they identified with.

How to support your child: For homework this coming week, encourage your child to pick a **R.A.K.** day. On this **R.A.K.** day your child should try to complete at least five acts from a given menu of **Random Acts of Kindness**. Assist your child in creating their own suggestions for what constitutes a **R.A.K.** Rate your own **R.A.K.** in order of preference from 1 to 5, highlighting to your child how it would make you feel and reminding them that your well-being is individual to you.

Lesson 7: Ingredient 4: Rainbow Moments

In this lesson children are introduced to the concept of *Rainbow Moments*. These moments relate to the little parts of our day where things go well for us, such as enjoying playing with a friend or noticing something beautiful in nature. It is explained to children that our brains naturally look for bad things in our day and with *Rainbow Moments*, we are re-training our brains to notice and pay attention to the small, simple, positive things that occur on a daily basis.

How to support your child: Discuss your child's *Rainbow Moments* in their Activity Book, exploring which of the positive emotions identified in Lesson 2 were experienced as a result. For homework, help your child to notice and record three *Rainbow Moments* each day this week.

Lesson 8: Ingredient 5: Healthy Body, Happy Mind

The final ingredient of our *Positive Emotion Potion - Healthy Body, Happy Mind* is discussed in this lesson. Children are presented with the idea that if we take care of our bodies and keep them healthy, it can help us to feel good and consequently help our well-being. There are three key elements to *Healthy Body, Happy Mind*: Eating Healthy Food (cutting down on junk foods), Moving our Bodies (one hour per day) and Getting Enough Sleep (ten hours for a child of their age).

How to support your child: Provide opportunities to support your child with these activities. If you are driving to school, park a distance away to allow your child to walk and have the benefit of additional exercise. Perhaps try a new vegetable or fruit each day. Encourage your child to participate in a calm bedtime routine to allow the transition into sleep to occur more easily. For each day, discuss any small changes made to the feeling your child experienced during that day. Were they feeling less tired and more positive?

Lesson 9: Positive Emotion Potion - Mix and Enjoy
Lesson 10: Review

In these lessons, children recall and revise each of the five ingredients of the *Positive Emotion Potion*. Children examine different scenarios of the ingredients learnt and relate each one to the *Positive Emotion Potion* and to improved well-being. Children will practise some or all of the ingredients as outlined in their homework. A *Well-Being Self-Assessment Check up* is included at the back of your child's *Positive Emotions Activity Book* for future reference, if your child needs to review this *Positive Emotions* course.

How to support your child: For homework in week nine, children are invited to see how many of the *Positive Emotion Potion* ingredients they can use each day and tick their tracker identifying their favourite ingredient. Discuss your own favourite ingredient in the *Positive Emotion Potion* with your child, reinforcing that positive emotions created for each person are individual and unique to them. Using the *Potion Tracker* in Lesson 10 (Review), children are encouraged to use some or all of the *Positive Emotion Potion* every day to support their well-being. Identifying their favourite ingredient, individual to them, is a key element of this activity.

Notes

Class Posters (CP)

A number of photocopiable class posters for displaying purposes during and after the delivery of this *Positive Emotions* programme have been included in this book and on the accompanying DVD. Each class poster has a CP reference as follows:

Lesson 1: What is Well-Being?
What Does Well-Being Mean? (CP1A – CP1G)

Lesson 2: Positive Emotions
Positivity Weighing Scales (CP2)

Lesson 4: Attitude of Gratitude
Attitude of Gratitude Poster (CP4)

Lesson 5: Feel-Good-Flow
Feel-Good-Flow Poster (CP5)

Lesson 6: Random Acts of Kindness
Random Acts of Kindness Poster (CP6)

Lesson 7: Rainbow Moments
Rainbow Moments Poster (CP7)

Lesson 8: Healthy Body, Happy Mind
Healthy Body Poster (CP8)

Lesson 9: Positive Emotion Potion - Mix and Enjoy
Positive Emotion Potion Ingredients (CP9)

What does well-being mean?

"Well-being means feeling good and strong in our minds and bodies, having energy, getting along with and helping others, knowing our strengths and feeling proud because we are doing our best. It means we can cope with the little problems and disappointments of life. It means enjoying life, being grateful for what we have and accepting ourselves just as we are!"

Weaving Well-Being - Positive Emotions - Teacher Resource Book by Fiona Forman & Mick Rock
© 2016 Outside The Box Learning Resources Ltd - www.otb.ie - Copying of this page permitted by purchasing school only.

CP1A

Well-being means

feeling good

in my body

and my mind!

Having energy

and fun!

CP1B

Well-being means getting on well with, and helping others!

Weaving Well-Being

THE MORE YOU WEAVE...
THE BETTER YOU FEEL!

CP1C

Well-being means knowing and using my strengths!

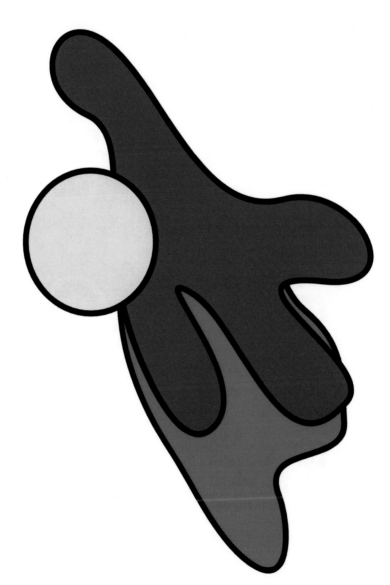

Weaving Well-Being
THE MORE YOU WEAVE...
THE BETTER YOU FEEL!

CP1D

79

Well-being means being able to cope with all the normal ups and downs of life!

CP1E

Well-being means enjoying life and feeling proud of doing my best!

CP1F

81

Well-being means feeling grateful and accepting myself just as I am!

CP1G

Positivity Weighing Scales

We need at least three Positive Emotions to balance one Negative Emotion!

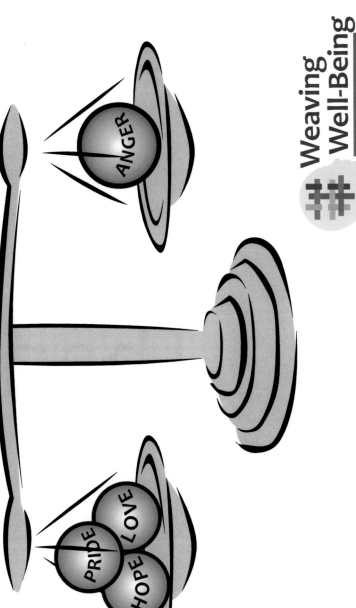

Weaving Well-Being - Positive Emotions - Teacher Resource Book by Fiona Forman & Mick Rock
© 2016 Outside The Box Learning Resources Ltd - www.otb.ie - Copying of this page permitted by purchasing school only.

CP2

Weaving Well-Being
THE MORE YOU WEAVE...
THE BETTER YOU FEEL!

Weaving Well-Being
THE MORE YOU WEAVE... THE BETTER YOU FEEL!

ATTITUDE OF GRATITUDE

An Attitude of Gratitude
reminds us to be thankful and appreciate
everything good in our lives.

Weaving Well-Being - Positive Emotions - Teacher Resource Book by Fiona Forman & Mick Rock
© 2016 Outside The Box Learning Resources Ltd - www.otb.ie - Copying of this page permitted by purchasing school only.

CP4

FEEL-GOOD-FLOW

Feel-Good-Flow
activities give us a challenge
and allow us to practise a skill.

CP5

Weaving Well-Being
THE MORE YOU WEAVE... THE BETTER YOU FEEL!

RANDOM ACTS OF KINDNESS

Through Random Acts of Kindness, we help others and also help ourselves.

CP6

RAINBOW MOMENTS

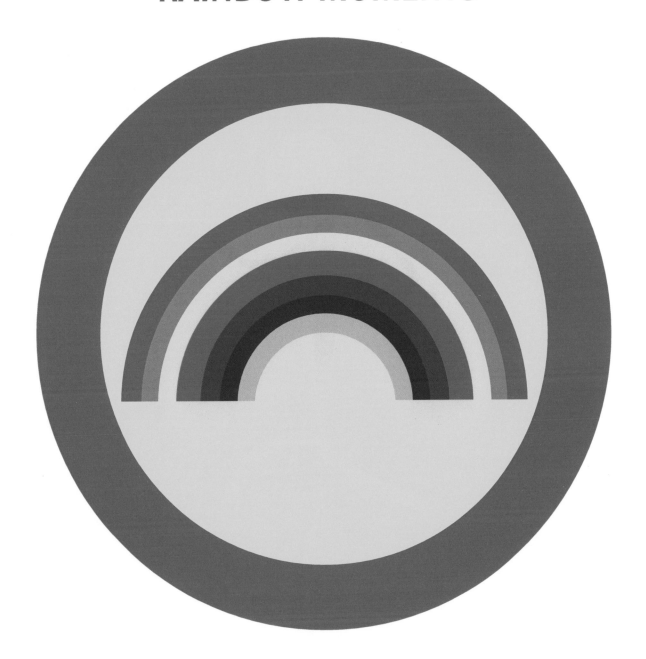

Rainbow Moments
give us a chance to train our minds to notice all the little positive parts of each day.

CP7

HEALTHY BODY

Healthy Body, Happy Mind reminds us that by keeping our bodies healthy, we can feel happier!

CP8

Positive Emotion Potion Ingredients
Mix and Enjoy!

CP9

89

Weaving Well-Being
THE MORE YOU WEAVE... THE BETTER YOU FEEL!

References

1. Park, N., & Peterson, C. (2008). Positive psychology and character strengths: Application to strengths-based school counselling. Professional School Counselling, 12(2), 85-92.

2. Green, H., McGinnity, A., Meltzer, H., Ford, T., & Goodman, R. (2005). Mental health of children and adolescents in Great Britain, 2004. ONS. The Stationery Office, London.

3. Pieris-Caldwell, I., Hotstone, C., & Eldridge, D. (2007). Young Australians: Their health and wellbeing 2007. Published by the Australian Institute of Health and Welfare & Printed by Pirion Pty Ltd, Canberra.

4. Health Service Executive (2014). Fifth Annual Child and Adolescent Mental Health Service Report 2012 - 2013. Dublin.

5. Seligman, M. E., Steen, T. A., Park, N., & Peterson, C. (2005). Positive psychology progress: empirical validation of interventions. American psychologist, 60(5), 410.

6. Fredrickson, B. L., & Branigan, C. (2005). Positive emotions broaden the scope of attention and thought action repertoires. Cognition & emotion, 19(3), 313-332.

7. Lyubomirsky, S., King, L., & Diener, E. (2005). The benefits of frequent positive affect: does happiness lead to success? Psychological bulletin, 131(6), 803.

8. Weare, K., & Nind, M. (2011). Mental health promotion and problem prevention in schools: what does the evidence say? Health promotion international, 26(suppl 1), i29-i69.

9. Stewart, D., Sun, J., Patterson, C., Lemerle, K., & Hardie, M. (2004). Promoting and building resilience in primary school communities: evidence from a comprehensive 'health promoting school' approach. International Journal of Mental Health Promotion, 6(3), 26-33.

10. Bizumic, B., Reynolds, K. J., Turner, J. C., Bromhead, D., & Subasic, E. (2009). The Role of the group in individual functioning: School identification and the psychological well being of staff and students. Applied Psychology, 58(1), 171-192.

11. Rutter, M., & Maughan, B. (2002). School effectiveness findings 1979–2002. Journal of school psychology, 40(6), 451-475.

12. Niemiec, C. P., & Ryan, R. M. (2009). Autonomy, competence, and relatedness in the classroom: Applying self-determination theory to educational practice. Theory and Research in Education, 7(2), 133-144.

13. Fredrickson, B. L. (2001). The role of positive emotions in positive psychology: The broaden-and-build theory of positive emotions. American psychologist, 56(3), 218.

14. Yang, H., Yang, S., & Isen, A. M. (2013). Positive affect improves working memory: Implications for controlled cognitive processing. Cognition & emotion, 27(3), 474-482.

15. Isen, A. M., Daubman, K. A., & Nowicki, G. P. (1987). Positive affect facilitates creative problem solving. Journal of personality and social psychology, 52(6), 1122.

16. Aron, A., Aron, E. N., & Smollan, D. (1992). Inclusion of Other in the Self Scale and the structure of interpersonal closeness. Journal of personality and social psychology, 63(4), 596.

Weaving Well-Being
THE MORE YOU WEAVE... THE BETTER YOU FEEL!

17. Fredrickson, B. L., Tugade, M. M., Waugh, C. E., & Larkin, G. R. (2003). What good are positive emotions in crisis? A prospective study of resilience and emotions following the terrorist attacks on the United States on September 11th, 2001. Journal of personality and social psychology, 84(2), 365.

18. Howell, R. T., Kern, M. L., & Lyubomirsky, S. (2007). Health benefits: Meta-analytically determining the impact of well-being on objective health outcomes. Health Psychology Review, 1(1), 83-136

19. Diener, E., Sandvik, E., & Pavot, W. (1991). Happiness is the frequency, not the intensity, of positive versus negative affect. Subjective well-being: An interdisciplinary perspective, 21, 119-139.

20. Overwalle, F. V., Mervielde, I., & Schuyter, J. D. (1995). Structural modelling of the relationships between attributional dimensions, emotions, and performance of college freshmen. Cognition & Emotion, 9(1), 59-85.

21. Froh, J. J., Sefick, W. J., & Emmons, R. A. (2008). Counting blessings in early adolescents: An experimental study of gratitude and subjective well-being. Journal of School Psychology, 46(2), 213-233.

22. McCullough, M. E., Emmons, R. A., & Tsang, J. A. (2002). The grateful disposition: a conceptual and empirical topography. Journal of personality and social psychology, 82(1), 112.

23. Csikszentmihalyi, M. (1997). Finding flow: The psychology of engagement with everyday life. Basic Books.

24. Shernoff, D. J., Csikszentmihalyi, M., Shneider, B., & Shernoff, E. S. (2003). Student engagement in high school classrooms from the perspective of flow theory. School Psychology Quarterly, 18(2), 158.

25. Lyubomirsky, S. (2008). The how of happiness: A scientific approach to getting the life you want. Penguin.

26. Sheldon, K. M., & Lyubomirsky, S. (2006). Achieving sustainable gains in happiness: Change your actions, not your circumstances*. Journal of Happiness Studies, 7(1), 55-86.

27. Seligman, M. E. (2012). Flourish: A visionary new understanding of happiness and well-being. Simon and Schuster, (84)

28. Baumeister, R. F., Bratslavsky, E., Finkenauer, C., & Vohs, K. D. (2001). Bad is stronger than good. Review of general psychology, 5(4), 323.

29. Dement, W. C. with C. VAUGHAN (1999/2000) The Promise of Sleep: The Scientific Connection Between Health, Happiness and a Good Night's Sleep.

30. Caspi, A., Sugden, K., Moffitt, T. E., Taylor, A., Craig, I. W., Harrington, H., & Poulton, R. (2003). Influence of life stress on depression: moderation by a polymorphism in the 5-HTT gene. Science, 301(5631), 386-389.

31. Levenson, R. W. (1994). Human emotion: A functional view. The nature of emotion: Fundamental questions, 123-126.

32. Frederickson, B. (2009). Positivity: Groundbreaking research reveals how to embrace the hidden strength of positive emotions, overcome negativity, and thrive. Crown Archetype, New York.

Weaving Well-Being

THE MORE YOU WEAVE... THE BETTER YOU FEEL!

Notes

Weaving Well-Being
THE MORE YOU WEAVE... THE BETTER YOU FEEL!

Notes

Weaving Well-Being
THE MORE YOU WEAVE... THE BETTER YOU FEEL!

Notes